MILK'S MICROWAVE COOKBOOK

Favourite Milk recipes
developed for the microwave
by Barb Holland

Published 1989

Published and distributed by:
The Ontario Milk Marketing Board
6780 Campobello Road
Mississauga, Ontario, Canada,
L5N 2L8

The Ontario Milk Marketing Board gratefully
acknowledges the co-operation and assistance of
Barb Holland in the development of this cookbook.

Designed by: Durkin, Rodgers and Battaglia Inc. Toronto, Ontario
Photography by: Douglas Bradshaw, Pat LaCroix, Philip Rostron, Robert Wigington
Typesetting by: Lettering Services Inc. Toronto, Ontario

Printed in Hong Kong

NATURAL GOODNESS MADE EASY

When it comes to microwaving, Milk is a natural. You can now enjoy the great taste and nutrition of Milk-based dishes without the bother of double boilers, scorched pans and clean-ups that were often a feature of conventional cooking.

When cooked in a microwave oven, Milk dishes retain all their moistness, flavour and nutrients, and cook in a fraction of the time.

Whether you're new to microwave cooking or an experienced chef, you'll find these recipes easy to follow and rewarding to taste. They were adapted for the microwave from the many editions of the Milk Calendar, as well as the *Cook Milk In Any Flavour You Like* Cookbook. Chosen for their appetite and family appeal, the recipes have been updated and streamlined to reflect today's tastes and ingredients. Most of the recipes serve four with top priority being given to timesaving convenience and delicious flavour.

Microwave cooking not only saves time, it allows you to cook with flair while preserving all the natural goodness found in Milk and other ingredients.

Wishing you many delicious, microwave meals.

Barb Holland

CONTENTS

Sauces

Pasta, Eggs and Cheese 97-120

Vegetables 123-137

THE BENEFITS OF MILK IN YOUR MICROWAVE

Microwaving makes the preparation of all Milk-based dishes faster and easier.

Since the microwave heats without drying, many Milk-based dishes can be made ahead of time and popped into the microwave at the last minute, for cooking or reheating.

Traditional favourites such as creamy baked custards, fluffy chiffons, rich puddings and pie fillings can all be made quickly, without the many steps involved in conventional cooking.

Because they're microwaved with a minimum of water, vegetable dishes retain more nutrients, texture, colour and flavour than in conventional cooking. They're not only faster, but with Milk, even more nutritious.

When it comes to Milk-based soups and sauces, microwave preparation ensures the elimination of lumps, scorching and constant stirring. As well, less fat is needed than in conventional cooking.

Not only is Milk a natural for microwave recipes, it complements the microwave in the preparation of everyday foods. For instance, hot chocolate couldn't be easier than just microwaving chocolate Milk or Milk with chocolate mix right in the mug. And Milk's natural goodness works wonders in the microwave with canned soups, hot cereals, and even pasta sauces.

When heating Milk in your microwave, be sure to give it a stir. It will help prevent a skin from forming on top and prevent uneven heating or boilovers. Because of the speed of microwave cooking, pressure from steam builds up rapidly. A quick stir will add air, slowing down the boiling process and minimizing the chance of a boilover.

RECIPE INGREDIENTS

Since time is an important consideration for most cooks, some of the ingredients used in these recipes have been selected to provide shortcuts, without sacrificing flavour. Chicken stock mix, frozen mixed vegetables, canned tomatoes, spaghetti sauce or packaged pudding and pie filling have been used because they are good quality products that cut down on both preparation and cooking times.

All the recipes were tested using 2% Milk, the most popular Milk among Canadians. You can substitute homogenized or skim Milk, if you prefer.

Where a recipe calls for flour, all-purpose flour was the one tested. Where sugar is mentioned, it refers to granulated white sugar, unless brown sugar or icing sugar are specified. Because microwave baked goods don't brown as well as in conventional baking, dark brown sugar is recommended in a few instances.

Most of the pasta recipes use dried pasta. If you prefer fresh, feel free to substitute, but increase the quantities and reduce the cooking time according to package instructions.

In most of the recipes calling for salt, it is suggested to season "to taste." This has been done to cut down on the amount of sodium and in recognition that tastes differ.

A WORD ABOUT MICROWAVE OVENS

All microwave ovens were not created equal. They vary in their cooking wattage, in the distribution of microwave energy, the size of the cavity and in other features.

The recipes in this cookbook were tested in 600 to 700 watt microwave ovens. If your oven has a lower wattage, give the recipe a little extra cooking time. A higher wattage oven will likely cook a little faster.

The guidelines given for cooking times are just that–guidelines. Use your sense of smell, taste, sight and feel, as well as the suggestions in each recipe to determine when a dish is done.

The recipes follow the standard terms and percentages determined by the International Microwave Power Institute (IMPI):

High (100%)
Medium-High (70%)
Medium (50%)
Medium-Low (30%)

Microwave oven manufacturers use different names for the various power levels. If you are unsure of the cooking wattage or power levels of your microwave oven, refer to its instruction manual or contact the manufacturer.

THE BASICS OF MICROWAVE COOKING

Microwave cooking has a lot in common with conventional cooking, but there are some fundamental differences. As with any new activity, you need to learn a few techniques and skills to do it well.

How Microwaves Cook

Microwaves penetrate the outer edges of food and are absorbed by the water, sugar and fat molecules in food. The absorbed energy causes the food molecules to move very rapidly. It is this activity which essentially cooks the food.

Cooking Time

Time is much more critical in microwave cooking than in conventional cooking. A few minutes longer in a conventional oven may not spoil a dish, but in a microwave, it can.

Many factors affect microwave cooking time. The amount of food, the size and shape of the foods and dishes, the composition of the food and the starting temperature can all affect cooking time.

Food Quantity

The more food you put in a microwave oven, the more time it takes to cook, because more microwave energy is needed. The amount of microwave energy put out by the oven is constant, except when you vary the power. If you increase the amount of food, you must increase the cooking time, too.

Size and Shape

Microwaves penetrate food from all sides, top and bottom. This means that similarly sized pieces of food will cook more evenly than randomly cut pieces. To get the best results, cut meat and vegetables into even-sized pieces before cooking. When baking potatoes, choose ones that are similar in size.

Because of the way a microwave cooks, round or ring-shaped dishes produce the most evenly cooked food. The denser a food is, the longer it will take to cook. However, since microwaves are attracted to sugar and fat, the more of these ingredients a dish contains, the faster it will cook.

Starting Temperature

As with conventional cooking, frozen or refrigerated food takes longer to cook than food at room temperature.

Stirring

Stirring is an important part of microwave cooking because it helps distribute the heated and non-heated parts. Luckily, microwave cooking usually requires less stirring than conventional cooking. For example, with sauces, a good whisk at the beginning, middle and end of cooking is generally enough to produce a smooth, creamy result. Soups, some casseroles, and vegetable dishes should all be stirred occasionally to make sure that they cook evenly and without boiling over.

Rotating

Generally, those dishes which cannot be stirred should be turned over or rotated during cooking. Turn over a roast or chicken pieces partway through cooking, to help them cook evenly.

Arrangement

Proper arrangement means less handling of a dish during cooking. Since microwaves penetrate the outer edges and are then conducted through the food, place those portions or foods which are thicker or denser towards the outer edges of a dish.

Arrange foods such as potatoes in a circle, with a few inches between each one and with the centre empty, to help them cook more quickly. Chicken pieces or chops will cook better if the meatier parts are on the outer edges of the dish. Arrange food in a single layer, instead of piling it high, to provide a larger surface area for the microwaves to cook more evenly.

Food Covering

Covering food in the microwave helps it cook more efficiently and prevents splattering. Generally, whatever food you would cover in conventional cooking, should be covered in the microwave. The covers of microwave dishes or even a microwavable dinner plate will help retain moisture, but microwavable plastic wrap also works well. Always turn back a small edge to allow the steam to escape and prevent boilovers.

Waxed or parchment paper can also be used, especially on casseroles, chicken parts, pork chops and pasta dishes. Since these papers don't cling to cooking containers, some steam will escape, preventing the food from becoming soggy.

Plain white (not recycled) paper towels absorb moisture and are therefore ideal for cooking bacon or reheating bread and pastry products, keeping the crust crispy.

Piercing

Foods with a skin or membrane, such as squash, sweet potatoes, apples, sausages, chicken or whole fish, should be pierced before cooking, to let the steam escape and prevent them from bursting.

Salt

Since salt attracts microwave energy, it tends to overcook areas where it lies on the surface. If you use salt, mix it in with the rest of the ingredients where it won't affect the cooking.

Shielding

Microwaves reflect off metal, so small pieces of foil placed on parts of a dish will prevent overcooking. However, if foil pieces are placed too close to the walls of the oven or another piece of foil [within 1 inch (2.5 cm)] arcing might occur. Arcing is a spark or discharge of electricity between two metal points. It looks like lightning or a blue spark in your microwave and is dangerous because it could start a fire or pit the walls of the oven. If it occurs, turn off your microwave oven immediately and remove the foil or piece of metal.

Standing Time

Food that has been microwaved continues to cook even after the power has been turned off. This carry-over is referred to as standing time. The length of standing time depends on how long food has been cooking, the power level used, plus the density and type of food. Large dense foods such as a roast or whole rutabaga should be wrapped or tented with foil during standing time, to help them cook through to the centre. Most items cooked covered, should be kept covered and simply left on the counter during standing time.

Microwave Cookware

New technology often requires new tools. But many of the dishes and utensils you need are already in your cupboard. Heat-resistant glass, glass-ceramic, pottery, earthenware, stoneware and china cookware and dinnerware are all ideal for the microwave oven.

The Microwave Test

To find out how suitable your current dishes are, first of all check that they don't have a metallic trim (gold or silver) that could cause arcing in the microwave. (See the section on Shielding). Next, test each dish by placing it in the microwave beside a glass measure filled with 1 cup (250 mL) water. Make sure the dish and measure don't touch. Microwave at High (100%) for 1 minute, then check the dish. If it is cool, then it's suitable for use in the microwave. But if it feels quite warm, it's absorbing too much microwave energy, and shouldn't be used.

Plastic Dishes

Not all plastics are suitable for microwave use. Storage containers such as those used for yogurt or ice cream were never intended for microwave cooking temperatures, and shouldn't be used.

However, now there's a wide range of plastic cookware on the market designed for microwave use. It even goes from freezer-to-microwave-to-table-to-dishwasher, making the whole food preparation process easier. Lightweight, durable and reasonably priced, the cookware comes in a wide variety of shapes and sizes.

The Microwave Cupboard

Although you probably aren't short on cookware, here are some dishes and implements you'll find particularly useful in microwaving:

- Casseroles in 4, 6, 8 and 12 cup (1, 1.5, 2 or 3 L) sizes, preferably round, made from any of the recommended materials. Choose the size appropriate to the number of people you usually cook for.
- At least one shallow microwavable dish, such as an 11 x 7 inch (2 L) or 12 x 8 inch (3 L), that fits your microwave oven. Watch out for handles that can get in the way.

- Glass measures in varying sizes are perfect as microwave saucepans, since they are round and have a pouring spout and handle. The clear glass lets you keep track of the cooking process. The 8 cup (2 L) size is ideal for making soups, with enough space for them to simmer without boiling over.
- A durable microwavable plastic whisk or slotted spoon is useful and can be left in the dish between stirrings.
- A microwave roasting rack, bacon rack or trivet, usually made of microwavable plastic, is ideal for bacon, roasts and other meats.

APPETIZERS

Caesar Salad with
Creamy Garlic Dressing

Pork, Chicken and Ham Paté

Appetizers

Whether you're preparing finger foods for a cocktail party, a starter for a dinner party or just a snack for the family, the microwave can cut down on both the effort and the cooking time.

These recipes range from delicious dips for vegetables to sophisticated finger foods such as tiny salmon quiches, mushroom croustades and meatballs. Some, like the salad, make a light meal. Traditional dishes such as Coquilles St. Jacques are particularly tender when cooked in a microwave, and a smooth fondue like Gouda Dunk is perfect for casual entertaining.

MEXICAN CHEESE DIP

A spicy dip for tortilla chips or raw vegetables. This dip reheats well, making it an ideal make-ahead.

2 tbsp.	butter	30 mL
1	small onion, chopped	1
1	clove garlic, minced	1
1-2 tbsp.	chopped fresh jalapeno or chili peppers	15-30 mL
2 tbsp.	flour	30 mL
1 cup	Milk	250 mL
1	medium sized, ripe tomato, chopped	1
1 cup	shredded Cheddar cheese tortilla chips or raw vegetables	250 mL

1. Combine butter, onion, garlic and peppers in a 4 cup (1 L) micro-wavable casserole. Microwave, uncovered, at High (100%) for 2 to 3 minutes or until softened.

2. Blend in flour and microwave at High (100%) for 30 seconds. Gradually whisk in Milk until smooth. Add tomatoes, cover and microwave at High (100%) for 3 to 5 minutes or until mixture comes to a boil and thickens. Whisk at least once during cooking.

3. Stir in cheese until melted. Serve warm with tortilla chips or raw vegetables as dippers.

4. If making ahead, cool, then cover and refrigerate. To serve, reheat, covered, at High (100%) for 2 to 3 minutes, or until warm. Stir twice.

Makes 2 cups (500 mL).

Note: If using fresh jalapeno or chili peppers, soften along with onion and garlic. If using canned or bottled peppers, add with the cheese at the end.

GOUDA DUNK

A smooth cheese fondue such as this one can be prepared easily in the microwave with no sticky pots to worry about.

2 tbsp.	butter	30	mL
2	green onions, chopped	2	
2 tbsp.	flour	30	mL
2 tsp.	chicken stock mix	10	mL
1 1/2 cups	Milk	375	mL
1/2 tsp.	Worcestershire sauce	2	mL
2 1/2 cups	shredded Gouda cheese	625	mL
1 tbsp.	chopped fresh parsley	15	mL
	cubed bread, bread sticks		
	assorted raw vegetables, trimmed		
	(broccoli, cauliflower, mushrooms,		
	zucchini, red and green peppers, snow peas)		

1. Combine butter and green onions in an 8 cup (2 L) microwavable casserole. Microwave, uncovered, at High (100%) for 1 minute or until softened.

2. Blend in flour and chicken stock mix and microwave at High (100%) for 30 seconds. Gradually whisk in Milk until smooth. Add Worcestershire sauce. Cover and microwave at High (100%) for 3 to 5 minutes or until mixture comes to a boil and thickens. Whisk at least once during cooking.

3. Stir in cheese until melted. If necessary, cover and microwave at Medium (50%) for 1 to 2 minutes or until cheese completely melts.

4. Stir in parsley. Use long handled forks to dip bread cubes and vegetables into fondue. If mixture cools down, reheat at Medium (50%), or keep warm over a burner.

Makes about 4 cups (1 L), 6 appetizer servings.

HONEY GARLIC MEATBALLS

These not only reheat well, but freeze well too, making them an ideal make-ahead appetizer. A microwave rack is essential to prevent meatballs from steaming in their own moisture and helps them to brown nicely.

1 1/2 lbs.	lean ground beef	750	g
3/4 cup	fine dry breadcrumbs	175	mL
1/2 cup	Milk	125	mL
1	onion, finely chopped	1	
1	egg, lightly beaten	1	
1 tsp.	Worcestershire sauce	5	mL
1/2 tsp.	salt	2	mL
1/4 tsp.	pepper	1	mL
Sauce			
1 tbsp.	butter	15	mL
4	cloves garlic, minced	4	
3/4 cup	ketchup	175	mL
1/2 cup	honey	125	mL
1/4 cup	soy sauce	50	mL
1/4 cup	water	50	mL

1. Combine beef, breadcrumbs, Milk, onion, egg, Worcestershire sauce, salt and pepper. Mix well and shape into 1 inch (2.5 cm) balls.

2. Arrange 1/3 of meatballs (about 18) evenly on a microwave roasting rack about 1/2 inch (1 cm) apart. Cover with waxed paper and micro-wave at High (100%) for 3 to 5 minutes or until no longer pink. Rotate rack or rearrange meatballs, as necessary, partway through for even cooking. Transfer meatballs to an 8 cup (2 L) microwavable casserole.

3. Pour excess fat off rack and repeat with remaining meatballs in two more batches.

4. To make sauce, combine butter and garlic in a 4 cup (1 L) glass measure or microwavable casserole. Microwave, uncovered, at High (100%) for 1 minute or until softened and fragrant. Stir in ketchup, honey, soy sauce and water. Microwave, uncovered, at High (100%) for 2 to 3 minutes or until mixture comes to a boil. Stir at least once during cooking. Pour over meatballs and stir well to coat evenly.

5. If serving immediately, cover and microwave at High (100%) for 2 to 5 minutes or until warm. Serve with cocktail picks.

Makes about 48 meatballs.

SALMON TARTS

Use frozen tart shells for these mini quiches to save time. Bake shells conventionally for a toasty colour and flavour.

24	2 inch (5 cm) baked tart shells	24
1 cup	Milk	250 mL
1	7 1/2 oz. (213 g) can salmon, drained and flaked	1
1 cup	shredded Swiss cheese	250 mL
3	green onions, chopped	3
1 tbsp.	chopped fresh parsley	15 mL
1 tbsp.	flour	15 mL
1/4 tsp.	salt	1 mL
1/4 tsp.	pepper	1 mL
	few drops of Tabasco sauce	
3	eggs	3

1. Measure Milk into a 1 cup (250 mL) glass measure and microwave at High (100%) for 2 minutes or until warm. Set aside.

2. In a medium bowl, thoroughly combine salmon, cheese, onions, parsley, flour, salt, pepper and Tabasco. In a small bowl, lightly beat eggs and gradually pour in warm Milk, whisking constantly. Add to salmon mixture and blend well.

3. Arrange 6 baked tart shells in a ring formation on a microwave roasting rack. The rack will prevent pastry from getting soggy. Spoon about 2 tbsp. (30 mL) of filling into each shell. Microwave, uncovered, at Medium (50%) for 4 to 6 minutes or until filling is just set. Rotate rack, if necessary, partway through to ensure even cooking. Remove from rack and cool. Repeat with remaining tarts, 6 at a time.

Makes 24 tarts.

CREOLE CRAB ON PATTY SHELLS

Serve this colourful appetizer over baked patty shells (also known as vol-au-vent). If you like it spicier, add Tabasco sauce.

2 tbsp.	butter	30	mL
1/2 cup	chopped green pepper	125	mL
1	onion, chopped	1	
1	clove garlic, minced	1	
2 tbsp.	flour	30	mL
1/2 tsp.	dry mustard	2	mL
1/4 tsp.	cayenne	1	mL
	salt and pepper		
1 cup	Milk	250	mL
2 tbsp.	tomato paste	30	mL
1	4.23 oz. (120 g) can crab meat, drained and flaked	1	
1 tsp.	lemon juice	5	mL
6	baked patty shells (vol-au-vent)	6	
2 tbsp.	chopped fresh parsley	30	mL

1. Combine butter, green pepper, onion and garlic in a 6 cup (1.5 L) microwavable casserole. Microwave, uncovered, at High (100%) for 2 to 4 minutes or until vegetables are softened.

2. Blend in flour, dry mustard, cayenne and a pinch each of salt and pepper. Microwave, uncovered, at High (100%) for 30 seconds. Gradually whisk in Milk, then tomato paste and blend until smooth. Cover and microwave at High (100%) for 3 to 5 minutes or until mixture comes to a boil and thickens. Whisk at least once during cooking.

3. Stir in crab meat, lemon juice and salt and pepper to taste. Spoon over patty shells and garnish each with parsley.

Serves 6.

MUSHROOM CROUSTADES

Croustades are bite-size toast cups. They can be made well ahead and stored in an airtight container, but make the filling just before serving so it is warm. Try to buy sandwich bread which has thinner slices.

18	slices fresh, sandwich bread (1 loaf)	18	
1 tbsp.	butter	15	mL
2 cups	finely chopped mushrooms	500	mL
2	green onions, chopped	2	
2	cloves garlic, minced	2	
1 tbsp.	chopped fresh parsley	15	mL
1 tsp.	lemon juice	5	mL
1/2 tsp.	dried tarragon	2	mL
	salt and pepper		
1 tbsp.	butter	15	mL
2 tbsp.	flour	30	mL
1/2 cup	Milk	125	mL
1 tbsp.	sour cream	15	mL
	chopped fresh parsley		

1. To make croustades, cut a 3 inch (8 cm) round from each bread slice. With a rolling pin, roll very flat. Fit 6 into a microwave muffin pan. Microwave, uncovered, at High (100%) for 1 1/2 to 2 1/2 minutes or until dry and lightly toasted in spots. Watch carefully, as they can easily burn. Rotate pan, as necessary, during cooking. Remove cups immediately and turn upside down on counter to cool and crisp. Wipe muffin pan dry with a tea towel and repeat with remaining bread.

2. Combine butter, mushrooms, green onions and garlic in a 6 cup (1.5 L) microwavable casserole. Microwave, uncovered, at High (100%) for 4 to 6 minutes or until mushrooms are very tender. Stir once during cooking. Add parsley, lemon juice, tarragon and salt and pepper to taste. Set aside.

3. Melt butter in a 2 cup (500 mL) glass measure at High (100%) for 20 to 30 seconds. Blend in flour and microwave at High (100%) for 30 seconds. Gradually stir in Milk until smooth. Microwave, uncovered, at High (100%) for 1 1/2 to 3 minutes or until mixture comes to a boil and thickens. Stir at least once.

4. Stir into mushroom mixture until smooth. Add sour cream, blending well. Spoon filling into croustades. Garnish each with a little chopped parsley and serve immediately.

Makes 18.

COQUILLES ST. JACQUES

A delicious and simple appetizer that you can make ahead. Buy the scallops fresh from a reliable source and do not overcook these delicate morsels.

1/4 cup	butter, divided	50	mL
3	green onions, chopped	3	
2 tbsp.	chopped fresh parsley	30	mL
1/2 tsp.	dried tarragon	2	mL
16	medium sea scallops, about 1/2 lb. (250 g)	16	
1/4 cup	dry white wine	50	mL
2 tbsp.	flour	30	mL
2/3 cup	Milk (approx.)	150	mL
	salt and pepper		
1/2 cup	toasted, buttered breadcrumbs*	125	mL
2 tbsp.	grated Parmesan cheese	30	mL

1. Combine 2 tbsp. (30 mL) of the butter, green onions, parsley and tarragon in a shallow microwavable dish such as a glass pie plate. Microwave, uncovered, at High (100%) for 1 to 2 minutes or until softened.

2. Rinse scallops under cold water and pat dry with paper towels. Add to butter mixture, stirring to coat evenly. Pour wine over and cover with vented plastic wrap. Microwave at Medium-High (70%) for 4 to 6 minutes, or just until opaque. Do not overcook. Stir gently partway through cooking. Uncover and set aside.

3. Melt remaining butter in a 2 cup (500 mL) glass measure at High (100%) for 30 to 50 seconds. Blend in flour and microwave, uncovered, at High (100%) for 30 seconds. Gradually whisk in poaching liquid from scallops and enough Milk to make 1 1/4 cups (300 mL). Microwave, uncovered, at High (100%) for 3 to 5 minutes or until sauce comes to a boil and thickens. Whisk at least once during cooking. Season to taste with salt and pepper.

4. Place 4 scallops in each of 4 lightly buttered scallop shells or shallow microwavable dishes, about 4 1/2 inches (11 cm) in diameter. Divide sauce between shells. Combine breadcrumbs and Parmesan cheese; sprinkle evenly over scallop mixture. Arrange in a circle in microwave oven. Microwave, uncovered, at High (100%) for 1 1/2 to 2 minutes or just until sauce begins to bubble around the edges. Serve immediately.

Continued on next page

COQUILLES ST. JACQUES

(Continued)

5. If preparing ahead, refrigerate after sprinkling with crumbs. Just before serving, microwave at High (100%) for 2 to 3 minutes or until sauce starts to bubble.

Serves 4.

*To toast breadcrumbs, melt 2 tsp. (10 mL) butter in a shallow microwavable dish such as a glass pie plate at High (100%) for 20 to 30 seconds. Stir in 1/2 cup (125 mL) fresh breadcrumbs, coating with butter. Microwave, uncovered, at High (100%) for 2 to 4 minutes or until lightly golden and quite dry. Stir often to break up and prevent scorching. Let stand until cool. (They will crisp up during standing time.)

CRAB OR LOBSTER ON MELON

Slices of ripe melon provide a refreshing and colourful contrast to the seafood.

2 tbsp.	butter	30	mL
1	clove garlic, minced	1	
2 tbsp.	flour	30	mL
1/8 tsp.	cayenne	0.5	mL
1 cup	Milk	250	mL
1 cup	shredded mozzarella cheese	250	mL
1	4.23 oz. (120 g) can crab meat or lobster, drained and flaked	1	
2 tbsp.	chopped fresh chives	30	mL
2 tbsp.	chopped fresh parsley	30	mL
	salt and pepper		
1	ripe melon or cantaloupe, peeled and thinly sliced	1	
6	lemon wedges	6	

1. Combine butter and garlic in a 4 cup (1 L) microwavable bowl or casserole. Microwave, uncovered, at High (100%) for 1 to 2 minutes or until softened.

2. Blend in flour and cayenne and microwave at High (100%) for 30 seconds. Gradually stir in Milk until smooth. Cover and microwave at High (100%) for 3 to 5 minutes or until sauce comes to a boil and thickens. Stir at least once during cooking.

3. Stir in cheese until melted. Add crab meat, chives, and parsley. Season to taste with salt and pepper. Spoon over thin slices of melon. Garnish each with a lemon wedge.

Serves 6.

PORK, CHICKEN AND HAM PATÉ

This firm textured paté slices well when cold. Make one to two days before serving to completely cool and for flavours to develop. Ideal for a picnic, sandwich or a casual appetizer.

1 lb.	ground chicken or boneless, skinless chicken breasts	500 g
6 oz.	cooked ham, ground	170 g
1 lb.	ground pork	500 g
3	green onions, chopped	3
1 tbsp.	chopped fresh parsley	15 mL
1 tsp.	salt	5 mL
1/2 tsp.	pepper	2 mL
1/2 tsp.	dried thyme	2 mL
1/4 tsp.	allspice	1 mL
2	eggs, lightly beaten	2
1 cup	Milk	250 mL
1 cup	fresh breadcrumbs	250 mL

1. If you cannot find ground chicken, grind chicken breasts in food processor, as well as ham. Combine all ingredients well in a large bowl.

2. Pack firmly into a 9 x 5 inch (2 L) glass loaf pan. Place pan in another shallow microwavable dish (to catch drippings during cooking) and cover with waxed paper. Microwave at Medium-High (70%) for 35 to 40 minutes or until firm in centre. Rotate dish, 2-3 times, during cooking.

3. Let stand, covered, for 30 minutes. Remove from dish, scrape off fat; wrap well and refrigerate until using.

4. To serve, slice thinly when cold, and let stand at room temperature for 20 minutes before serving to take the chill off the paté. Serve with French bread, zesty mustard and gerkins.

Serves 10 to 16.

CLAM IMPERIAL

A starter to a meal that stretches clams a long way.

2 tbsp.	butter	30	mL
1	onion, chopped	1	
1	clove garlic, minced	1	
3 tbsp.	flour	45	mL
	salt and pepper		
1 cup	Milk	250	mL
1/2 tsp.	dried oregano	2	mL
1/2 cup	frozen whole kernel corn or peas	250	mL
1	5 oz. (142 g) can clams, undrained	1	
8	baked patty shells (vol-au-vent) or slices buttered toast	8	
	paprika		

1. Combine butter, onion and garlic in a 6 cup (1.5 L) microwavable casserole. Microwave, uncovered, at High (100%) for 2 to 3 minutes or until softened.

2. Blend in flour and a pinch each of salt and pepper and microwave, uncovered, at High (100%) for 30 seconds. Gradually whisk in Milk and oregano until smooth. Cover and microwave at High (100%) for 3 to 5 minutes or until sauce comes to a boil and thickens. Whisk at least once during cooking.

3. Stir frozen corn or peas into warm mixture, blending well. Add clams with their juice. Cover and microwave at High (100%) for 3 to 4 minutes or until heated through. Stir once during cooking. Season to taste with salt and pepper. Spoon over patty shells or toast. Sprinkle each with paprika.

Serves 8.

CAESAR SALAD WITH CREAMY GARLIC DRESSING

Store any leftover dressing in refrigerator for one week and use for potato, pasta or chicken salads.

1 tbsp.	dry mustard	15	mL
1 1/2 tbsp.	flour	20	mL
1 tsp.	salt	5	mL
1/4 tsp.	pepper	1	mL
2 cups	Milk	500	mL
2	egg yolks, lightly beaten	2	
1 tsp.	Worcestershire sauce	5	mL
1/4 tsp.	Tabasco sauce	1	mL
2	cloves garlic, minced	2	
3	anchovy fillets, minced or 1 tsp. (5 mL) anchovy paste	3	
1/3 cup	red wine vinegar	75	mL
1/3 cup	olive oil	75	mL
1	head Romaine lettuce	1	
4	slices bacon, cooked crisp and crumbled	4	
1 cup	croutons	250	mL
1/2 cup	grated Parmesan cheese	125	mL

1. Combine mustard, flour, salt and pepper in an 8 cup (2 L) glass measure or microwavable casserole. Gradually whisk in Milk until smooth. Microwave at High (100%) for 4 to 6 minutes or until mixture comes to a boil and thickens. Whisk twice during cooking.

2. Stir a small amount of hot mixture into lightly beaten egg yolks. Pour warmed yolks back into mixture, whisking constantly. Microwave, uncovered, at Medium (50%) for 1 to 2 minutes or until thickened. Whisk every 30 seconds.

3. Stir in Worcestershire, Tabasco, garlic, anchovies, vinegar and oil. Cool, then cover and refrigerate until ready to use. Just before serving, season with salt and pepper to taste.

4. Wash and dry lettuce. Break into bite-sized pieces. Just before serving, toss with enough dressing to coat leaves well. Sprinkle with bacon, croutons and cheese. Toss well.

Serves 6 to 8.

SPICY SHRIMP

Delicious, colourful and just a little spicy, these will be a hit when you need an appetizer at a cocktail party or a nibble before dinner.

1 lb.	medium raw shrimp, peeled and deveined	500	g
2 tbsp.	butter	30	mL
1	onion, chopped	1	
1/2 cup	chopped green pepper	125	mL
1	clove garlic, minced	1	
2 tbsp.	flour	30	mL
1 tsp.	curry powder	5	mL
1/2 tsp.	ground cumin	2	mL
1/4 tsp.	hot red pepper flakes	1	mL
1 cup	Milk	250	mL
1 tbsp.	lemon juice	15	mL
2 tbsp.	chopped fresh parsley salt and pepper	30	mL

1. Rinse peeled and deveined shrimp and set aside. Shrimp are delicate and very quick cooking, so take care not to overcook, particularly if making ahead to reheat later.

2. Combine butter, onion, green pepper and garlic in an 8 cup (2 L) microwavable casserole. Microwave, uncovered, at High (100%) for 2 to 3 minutes or until vegetables are softened.

3. Blend in flour, curry powder, cumin and red pepper flakes. Microwave, uncovered, at High (100%) for 30 seconds. Gradually whisk in Milk until smooth. Cover and microwave at High (100%) for 3 to 5 minutes or until mixture comes to a boil and thickens. Whisk at least once during cooking.

4. Gently but thoroughly stir shrimp into sauce. Cover and microwave at High (100%) for 3 to 4 minutes or until shrimp are just pink. Stir at least once during cooking to move cooked shrimp to centre of dish.

5. Stir in lemon juice and parsley. Let stand, covered, for a few minutes. Season to taste with salt and pepper. Serve warm with cocktail picks.

6. If making ahead, cool, then cover and refrigerate. Reheat, covered, at Medium-High (70%) for 4 to 6 minutes or until warm. Stir often.

About 30 shrimp, 6 to 8 appetizer servings.

SALMON AND DILL MOUSSE

This lighter version uses Milk rather than sour cream or cream cheese. Make a few hours or the day before to allow time to set.

1	envelope unflavoured gelatin	1
1 cup	Milk	250 mL
1	7 1/2 oz. (213 g) can salmon	1
3	green onions, finely chopped	3
1 tbsp.	lemon juice	15 mL
2 tsp.	horseradish	10 mL
1 tsp.	dried dill weed	5 mL
	Tabasco sauce	
	pepper	
	lemon slices, crackers or thin pumpernickel bread	

1. Sprinkle gelatin over Milk in a 2 cup (500 mL) glass measure. Let stand a few minutes to soften; stir. Microwave, uncovered, at High (100%) for 2 to 3 minutes or until gelatin is completely dissolved. Stir partway through.

2. Discard bones and skin from salmon but retain juices. Place in a medium bowl and mash. Add green onions, lemon juice, horseradish, dill weed, a few drops of Tabasco and pepper to taste. Mix well.

3. Pour Milk and gelatin mixture over all and blend well. Pour into a 2 cup (500 mL) mould or bowl. Cover and chill several hours or overnight until set.

4. If unmoulding, loosen edges with a knife and dip mould in warm water for a few seconds. Jiggle and invert onto serving plate. If not unmoulding, remove from refrigerator about 20 minutes before serving. Garnish with lemon slices, and serve with crackers or thin pumpernickel bread.

Serves 6 to 8.

CHICKEN SATAYS WITH PINEAPPLE PEANUT SAUCE

Satays, originally from southeast Asia, are popular appetizers that adapt well to the microwave. Simply cut pieces evenly and rearrange during cooking.

1 lb.	boneless, skinless chicken breasts	500	g
Marinade			
1/4 cup	oil	50	mL
1/4 cup	soy sauce	50	mL
2 tbsp.	lemon juice	30	mL
1 tsp.	sugar	5	mL
Pineapple Peanut Sauce			
1 cup	Milk	250	mL
1/2 cup	shredded coconut	125	mL
2 tbsp.	butter	30	mL
1	onion, chopped	1	
1	clove garlic, minced	1	
1 tsp.	curry powder	5	mL
1/2 tsp.	ground ginger	2	mL
1/2 cup	drained, crushed pineapple	125	mL
1/4 cup	crunchy peanut butter	50	mL

1. Trim any fat off chicken and cut into 3/4 inch (2 cm) pieces. Combine marinade in bowl just large enough to hold chicken pieces. Toss chicken in mixture, cover and marinate in refrigerator for at least one hour or as long as overnight.

2. Meanwhile to make sauce, microwave Milk at High (100%) for 2 minutes or until warm. Pour over coconut and let stand 15 minutes.

3. Combine butter, onion and garlic in a 4 cup (1 L) glass measure or microwavable casserole. Microwave, uncovered, at High (100%) for 2 to 3 minutes or until softened. Stir in curry and ginger. Add Milk mixture, pineapple and peanut butter. Cover and microwave at High (100%) for 3 to 5 minutes or until sauce comes to a boil and thickens. Stir at least once during cooking. Set aside.

4. Thread chicken pieces on 6 bamboo skewers, leaving a small space between each piece for even cooking. Arrange on a microwave roasting rack, spacing out evenly. Cover with waxed paper and microwave at Medium-High (70%) for 6 to 8 minutes or until tender and no longer pink. Turn over and rearrange skewers partway through cooking. Serve with warm Pineapple Peanut Sauce.

Serves 6.

SOUPS AND SAUCES

Quick and Easy Dessert Sauces

Clam Chowder with
Bacon and Croutons

Soups and Sauces

Sauces are amazingly simple when made in the microwave using a glass measure. Just stir the ingredients well at the beginning, once partway through cooking, and again at the end, and you'll enjoy a smooth sauce every time. Using a microwavable whisk or slotted spoon that can be left in the sauce between stirs, will also help eliminate lumps.

You'll notice that many of the sauce recipes begin with a classic butter flour mixture called a roux. It's important that the roux be cooked before adding liquid, to eliminate a starchy flavour and ensure a smooth blend. Add the Milk to the roux gradually and thoroughly blend. Allow the sauce to boil, with a stir, during cooking to thicken it. Milk-based soups are perfect for the microwave because they do not burn easily. They cook quickly, reheat well, and many of the recipes here freeze well. Soup will defrost even faster if frozen in single portions. Stirring two or three times during cooking distributes the ingredients for even cooking and prevents boilovers.

To add extra appeal to your soups, add a garnish of chopped fresh herbs, lemon or orange peel, julienne strips of vegetables, grated cheese or a swirl of yogurt or sour cream.

HEARTY VEGETABLE CHOWDER

This hearty soup, chock full of vegetables and pasta, is ideally suited for chilly days. Serve with crusty bread and a salad.

2	slices bacon, diced	2	
1	onion, chopped	1	
1	10 oz. (284 mL) can beef broth	1	
1	14 oz. (398 mL) can spaghetti sauce	1	
1 cup	water	250	mL
1/4 tsp.	dried basil	1	mL
2 cups	frozen or fresh mixed vegetables	500	mL
1/2 cup	spiral shaped pasta	125	mL
2 cups	Milk	500	mL
2 tbsp.	flour	30	mL
	salt and pepper		
	grated Parmesan cheese, optional		

1. Place bacon in 12 cup (3 L) microwavable casserole. Microwave, uncovered, at High (100%) for 3 to 4 minutes or until crisp. Remove bacon with a slotted spoon and reserve.

2. Stir onion into bacon drippings and microwave, uncovered, at High (100%) for 2 to 3 minutes or until onion is softened.

3. Stir in beef broth, spaghetti sauce, water, basil, vegetables and pasta. Cover and microwave at High (100%) for 15 to 18 minutes or until pasta is cooked. Stir 3 times during cooking.

4. Combine Milk and flour until smooth, stir into mixture. Microwave, uncovered, at High (100%) for 4 to 6 minutes or until mixture comes to a boil and thickens. Stir at least once during cooking.

5. Let stand 5 minutes before serving. Season to taste with salt and pepper. Garnish with reserved bacon and Parmesan cheese.

Makes 7 cups (1.75 L)

POTATO AND CHEDDAR CHEESE SOUP

A creamy, rich soup—serve with a salad for a light dinner or substantial lunch.

2 tbsp.	butter	30 mL
1	onion, chopped	1
1	clove garlic, minced	1
3	medium potatoes, peeled and diced	3
1 1/2 cups	chicken stock or 1 1/2 tsp. (7 mL) chicken stock mix in 1 1/2 cups (375 mL) water	375 mL
1/4 tsp.	dried thyme	1 mL
1 1/2 cups	Milk	375 mL
1 1/2 cups	shredded Cheddar cheese	375 mL
	salt and pepper	
2 tbsp.	chopped fresh parsley	30 mL

1. Combine butter, onion and garlic in an 8 cup (2 L) glass measure or microwavable casserole. Microwave, uncovered, at High (100%) for 2 to 3 minutes or until onion is softened.

2. Add potatoes, chicken stock and thyme. Cover and microwave at High (100%) for 8 to 12 minutes or until potatoes are tender. Stir at least twice during cooking.

3. Purée half the mixture; return to dish. Stir in Milk, cover and microwave at High (100%) for 3 to 5 minutes or until heated through.

4. Stir in cheese until melted. Season to taste with salt and pepper. Garnish with parsley.

Makes about 5 cups (1.25 L).

BROCCOLI CHEESE SOUP

Broccoli, Milk and Cheddar cheese go together beautifully in this tasty soup. The more aged the cheese, the stronger the taste.

2 tbsp.	butter	30	mL
1	onion, chopped	1	
2 tbsp.	flour	30	mL
1 1/2 cups	chicken stock or 1 1/2 tsp. (7 mL) chicken stock mix in 1 1/2 cups (375 mL) water	375	mL
1	300 g package frozen chopped broccoli or 3 cups (750 mL) chopped fresh broccoli	1	
1/4 tsp.	pepper	1	mL
	salt		
1 1/2 cups	Milk	375	mL
1 1/2 cups	shredded Cheddar cheese	375	mL
1/4 tsp.	Tabasco sauce	1	mL
2 tbsp.	chopped fresh dill, parsley or chives	30	mL
1	red pepper, chopped, optional	1	

1. Combine butter and onion in a 12 cup (3 L) microwavable casserole. Microwave, uncovered, at High (100%) for 2 to 4 minutes or until onion is softened.

2. Blend in flour and microwave, uncovered, at High (100%) for 30 seconds. Gradually whisk in chicken stock until smooth. Add broccoli. Cover and microwave at High (100%) for 8 to 12 minutes or until broccoli is tender. Stir 2 or 3 times during cooking.

3. Purée mixture and return to dish. Add pepper, salt to taste, Milk, cheese and Tabasco. Cover and microwave at High (100%) for 3 to 5 minutes or until heated through and cheese is melted.

4. Let stand, covered, for 5 minutes before serving. Season to taste with salt and pepper. Garnish with fresh herb of your choice and red peppers, if desired.

Makes 6 cups (1.5 L).

AUTUMN VEGETABLE SOUP

A cornucopia of fall vegetables are in this hearty soup. If you like a chunky soup, purée only half the mixture.

2 tbsp.	butter	30	mL
1	onion, chopped	1	
2	stalks celery, chopped	2	
2	medium carrots, diced	2	
2	cloves garlic, minced	2	
1	small zucchini, chopped	1	
1	large potato, peeled and diced	1	
1	medium tomato, diced	1	
3 tbsp.	chopped fresh parsley or 1 tsp. (5 mL) dried, divided	45	mL
2 cups	chicken stock or 2 tsp. (10 mL) chicken stock mix or 2 cubes in 2 cups (500 mL) water	500	mL
1 tsp.	dried thyme	5	mL
1/2 tsp.	salt	2	mL
1/4 tsp.	pepper	1	mL
2 cups	Milk	500	mL

1. Combine butter, onion, celery, carrots and garlic in an 8 cup (2 L) glass measure or microwavable casserole. Microwave, uncovered, at High (100%) for 4 to 6 minutes or until vegetables are softened.

2. Add zucchini, potato, tomato, half the parsley, chicken stock, thyme, salt and pepper. Cover and microwave at High (100%) for 16 to 20 minutes or until potatoes are tender. Stir at least twice during cooking.

3. Purée all or half of mixture in food processor or blender. Return to dish. Stir in Milk, cover and microwave at High (100%) for 4 to 6 minutes or until heated through.

4. Let stand for 5 minutes before serving. Season to taste with salt and pepper. Garnish with remaining parsley.

Makes 6 cups (1.5 L).

CLAM CHOWDER WITH BACON AND CROUTONS

A thick, chunky chowder that makes a good lunch or light dinner. Tips for crisping bacon and making the croutons for the garnish are below.

2 tbsp.	butter	30 mL
1	onion, chopped	1
2	potatoes, peeled and diced	2
2 1/2 cups	Milk, divided	625 mL
2 tbsp.	flour	30 mL
1 tsp.	dried thyme	5 mL
2	5 oz. (142 g) cans clams, undrained	2
	salt and pepper	

Garnish

bacon bits
croutons
sliced green onions

1. Combine butter and onion in an 8 cup (2 L) glass measure or micro-wavable casserole. Microwave, uncovered, at High (100%) for 2 to 3 minutes or until onion is softened.

2. Stir in potatoes and 1/2 cup (125 mL) Milk. Cover and microwave at High (100%) for 8 to 10 minutes or until potatoes are tender. Stir partway through cooking.

3. Combine flour and remaining 2 cups (500 mL) Milk until smooth. Stir into potato mixture along with thyme and clams and their liquid. Cover and microwave at High (100%) for 12 to 14 minutes or until heated through. Stir 2 or 3 times during cooking.

4. Let stand 5 minutes before serving. Season to taste with salt and pepper. Garnish with bacon bits, croutons and green onions.

Makes 7 cups (1.75 L).

To make bacon bits: To cook bacon, arrange 6 slices of bacon evenly on microwave roasting rack. Cover with double thickness of paper towel and microwave at High (100%) for 4 to 6 minutes or until bacon is crisp. Change paper towel as necessary to help absorb excess fat. Crumble or chop into pieces.

To make croutons, melt 1 tbsp. (15 mL) butter in a shallow microwav-able dish such as a glass pie plate at High (100%) for 30 to 45 seconds. Toss 1 slice bread, crusts removed and cubed, in butter coating evenly. Microwave, uncovered, at High (100%) for 2 to 4 minutes or until crisp. Stir or shake dish often. (Croutons will continue to crisp up during standing time.)

BEAN AND BACON POTAGE

A no-fuss, hearty soup that's on the table in 20 minutes or less. Serve with brown bread and fresh fruit for dessert and you'll have a complete meal in no time at all.

2	slices bacon, diced	2
1	onion, chopped	1
2 tsp.	chicken stock mix or 2 chicken bouillon cubes, crushed	10 mL
2 cups	Milk	500 mL
1	19 oz. (540 mL) can baked beans	1
1 cup	shredded Cheddar cheese	250 mL
1 tsp.	Worcestershire sauce	5 mL
	salt and pepper	
2 tbsp.	chopped fresh parsley	30 mL

1. Combine bacon and onion in an 8 cup (2 L) glass measure or micro-wavable casserole. Microwave, uncovered, at High (100%) for 2 to 3 minutes or until onion is tender and bacon cooked.

2. Blend in chicken stock mix, then Milk, beans, cheese and Worcestershire sauce. Cover and microwave at High (100%) for 6 to 8 minutes or until cheese is melted and soup is heated through. Stir twice during cooking.

3. Purée in food processor or blender until smooth. Reheat, if necessary, before serving. Season to taste with salt and pepper. Garnish with parsley.

Makes 5 cups (1.25 L).

CREOLE FISH BISQUE

This is a chunky and colourful soup, hearty enough for a meal. If using frozen fish, cut it up without thawing and add 2 to 3 minutes to the cooking time.

2 tbsp.	butter	30 mL
2 tbsp.	flour	30 mL
2 cups	Milk	500 mL
1	19 oz. (540 mL) can stewed tomatoes with onions and peppers	1
8 oz.	fish fillets, cut into 1 inch (2.5 cm) pieces	250 g
2	small zucchini, thinly sliced	2
1/2 tsp.	dried thyme	2 mL
1/4 tsp.	cayenne	1 mL
	salt and pepper	

1. Melt butter in an 8 cup (2 L) glass measure or microwavable casserole at High (100%) for 30 to 50 seconds.

2. Blend in flour and microwave, uncovered, for 30 seconds. Gradually whisk in Milk until smooth. Add tomatoes, mashing with a fork or potato masher. Then add fish, zucchini, thyme and cayenne. Cover and microwave at High (100%) for 12 to 16 minutes or until zucchini and fish are cooked. Stir at least twice during cooking.

3. Let stand, covered, for 5 minutes before serving. Season to taste with salt and pepper.

Makes 7 cups (1.75 L)

CORN CHOWDER

This simple but delicious soup with a very robust corn taste is ideal for casual meals. Keep the ingredients on hand for when you need something in a hurry.

2 slices	bacon, diced	2
1	onion, chopped	1
2 tbsp.	flour	30 mL
2 cups	Milk	500 mL
1	14 oz. (398 mL) can cream style corn	1
1	12 oz. (341 mL) can whole kernel corn, drained	1
	salt and pepper	
2 tbsp.	chopped fresh parsley	30 mL

1. Combine bacon and onion in an 8 cup (2 L) glass measure or microwavable casserole. Microwave, uncovered, at High (100%) for 3 to 4 minutes or until onion is tender and bacon is cooked.

2. Blend in flour and microwave at High (100%) for 30 seconds. Gradually whisk in Milk, cream corn and corn kernels until smooth. Cover and microwave at High (100%) for 8 to 10 minutes or until mixture comes to a boil. Whisk twice during cooking.

3. Let stand, covered, for 5 minutes before serving. Season to taste with salt and pepper. Garnish with parsley.

Makes 5 cups (1.25 L).

HERBED TOMATO BISQUE

Dried dill weed gives canned tomatoes a summery taste in this creamy tomato soup.

2 tbsp.	butter	30 mL
1	onion, chopped	1
1	clove garlic, minced	1
2 tbsp.	flour	30 mL
1 1/2 cups	Milk	375 mL
1	28 oz.(796 mL) can tomatoes, undrained	1
2 tbsp.	tomato paste*	30 mL
1 tsp.	dried dill weed	5 mL
1/2 tsp.	sugar	2 mL
	salt and pepper	

1. Combine butter, onion and garlic in an 8 cup (2 L) glass measure or microwavable casserole. Microwave, uncovered, at High (100%) for 2 to 3 minutes or until onion is softened.

2. Blend in flour and microwave, uncovered, at High (100%) for 30 seconds. Gradually whisk in Milk until smooth. Cover and microwave at High (100%) for 4 to 6 minutes or until mixture comes to a boil and thickens slightly. Whisk twice during cooking.

3. Add tomatoes and mash with a potato masher or fork. Stir in tomato paste, dill weed and sugar. Cover and microwave at High (100%) for 8 to 10 minutes or until mixture boils. Stir twice during cooking.

4. Let stand, covered, for 5 minutes before serving. Season to taste with salt and pepper. Garnish with a little sprinkle of dried dill weed.

Makes 5 cups (1.25 L).

* Freeze leftover tomato paste in 1 tbsp. (15 mL) amounts on waxed paper. When solid, transfer to an airtight freezer bag, label and return to freezer. Use when small amounts are needed in a recipe.

CREAM OF ASPARAGUS SOUP

When asparagus is plentiful, make this delightful soup —it is delicious hot or cold. If cold soup is too thick, thin with additional Milk.

1 lb.	fresh asparagus	500 g
1 cup	water	250 mL
2 tbsp.	butter	30 mL
1	onion, chopped	1
2 tbsp.	flour	30 mL
1 tbsp.	chicken stock mix	15 mL
2 cups	Milk	500 mL
	salt and pepper	

1. Snap off and discard tough stem ends of asparagus. Rinse well in cold water. Cut into 1 inch (2.5 cm) pieces. Place in an 8 cup (2 L) glass measure or microwavable casserole with the water. Cover and microwave at High (100%) for 8 to 10 minutes or until tender. Stir at least once during cooking. Reserve a few tips for garnish. Purée in food processor or blender until smooth. Set aside.

2. In same dish combine butter and onion. Microwave, uncovered, at High (100%) for 2 to 3 minutes or until onion is softened.

3. Blend in flour and chicken stock mix. Microwave, uncovered, at High (100%) for 30 seconds. Gradually whisk in asparagus purée and Milk until smooth. Cover and microwave at High (100%) for 9 to 12 minutes or until soup comes to a boil and thickens slightly. Whisk twice during cooking.

4. Let stand, covered, for 5 minutes before serving. Season to taste with salt and pepper. Garnish with reserved asparagus tips. If serving cold, cool to room temperature, then chill well.

Makes 4 cups (1 L).

CANADIANA CHEDDAR CHEESE SOUP

Use an old or sharp Cheddar cheese for a richly flavoured soup. For a different taste, try beer or ale instead of water.

2 tbsp.	butter	30	mL
1	onion, chopped	1	
1	clove garlic, minced	1	
3 tbsp.	flour	45	mL
1 tbsp.	chicken stock mix	15	mL
1/2 tsp.	paprika	2	mL
1/2 tsp.	dry mustard	2	mL
2 cups	shredded sharp Cheddar cheese	500	mL
2 cups	Milk	500	mL
1 cup	water	250	mL
	salt and pepper		
	sliced green onion tops or chives		

1. Combine butter, onion and garlic in an 8 cup (2 L) glass measure or microwavable casserole. Microwave, uncovered, at High (100%) for 2 to 3 minutes or until onion is tender.

2. Blend in flour, chicken stock mix, paprika and dry mustard. Microwave, uncovered, at High (100%) for 30 seconds. Gradually whisk in Milk and water until smooth. Cover and microwave at High (100%) for 8 to 10 minutes or until mixture comes to a boil and thickens. Whisk twice during cooking.

3. Stir in cheese until melted. Season to taste with salt and pepper. Garnish with sliced green onion tops or chives.

Makes 4 cups (1 L).

GOLDEN CARROT SOUP

Rice is the thickener in this colourful winter vegetable soup.

2 tbsp.	butter	30	mL
1	onion, chopped	1	
2 cups	thinly sliced carrots	500	mL
1 tbsp.	chicken stock mix, or	15	mL
	2 chicken bouillon cubes, crushed		
2 cups	hot water	500	mL
1/4 cup	uncooked long grain rice	50	mL
1/2 tsp.	salt	2	mL
1/4 tsp.	pepper	1	mL
2 cups	Milk	500	mL
3 tbsp.	chopped fresh parsley	45	mL

1. Combine butter, onion and carrots in an 8 cup (2 L) glass measure or microwavable casserole. Microwave, uncovered, at High (100%) for 4 to 6 minutes or until carrots are almost tender.

2. Stir in chicken stock mix, hot water, rice, salt and pepper. Cover and microwave at High (100%) for 12 to 14 minutes or until rice is cooked. Stir 2 or 3 times during cooking.

3. Purée in food processor or blender until smooth. Return to dish and stir in Milk. Cover and microwave at High (100%) for 4 to 6 minutes or until heated through. Stir twice during cooking.

4. Let stand, covered, for 5 minutes before serving. Season to taste with salt and pepper. Garnish with parsley.

Makes 5 cups (1.25 L).

CREAMY ITALIAN MINESTRONE

This is a hearty meal-in-a bowl soup. Serve with crusty bread.

1/2 cup	dried macaroni	125	mL
1	10 oz. (300 g) package frozen, chopped spinach	1	
1 tbsp.	butter	15	mL
1	small zucchini, diced	1	
1	10 oz. (284 mL) can beef broth	1	
1	19 oz. (540 mL) can stewed tomatoes	1	
2 tbsp.	tomato paste	30	mL
1/2 tsp.	dried basil	2	mL
1/2 tsp.	dried oregano	2	mL
1/4 tsp.	garlic powder	1	mL
	salt and pepper		
1 1/2 cups	Milk	375	mL
	grated Parmesan cheese, optional		

1. Cook macaroni conventionally according to package directions. Drain and set aside.

2. While pasta is cooking, remove spinach from package. Wrap a piece of foil smoothly around half the block. Place on a microwavable plate. Microwave at Defrost (30%) for 6 to 8 minutes or until exposed spinach is thawed. Do not let foil touch oven walls. Cut block in half, rewrap and freeze or refrigerate the still-frozen spinach for another use. Drain thawed spinach well, squeezing out excess moisture and chop finely.

3. Combine butter and zucchini in an 8 cup (2 L) glass measure or micro-wavable casserole. Microwave, uncovered, at High (100%) for 2 to 4 minutes or until softened.

4. Stir in spinach, broth, tomatoes, tomato paste, basil, oregano, garlic powder and a pinch each of salt and pepper. Cover and microwave at High (100%) for 8 to 10 minutes or until soup comes to a boil. Stir at least twice during cooking.

5. Add Milk and pasta, cover and microwave at High (100%) for 3 to 5 minutes or until heated through.

6. Let stand, covered, for 5 minutes before serving. Season to taste with salt and pepper. Garnish each bowl with Parmesan cheese, if desired.

Makes 6 cups (1.5 L).

MUSHROOM AND LEEK SOUP

A creamy soup that is rich in flavour and texture without adding cream.

1/4 cup	butter	50 mL
3	small leeks, white part only, washed well and sliced	3
8 oz.	mushrooms, thinly sliced	250 g
1/4 cup	flour	50 mL
1/2 tsp.	salt	2 mL
1/4 tsp.	white pepper	1 mL
2 cups	Milk	500 mL
1 cup	chicken stock or 1 tsp. (5 mL) chicken stock mix in 1 cup (250 mL) water	250 mL
1 tbsp.	lemon juice or dry sherry	15 mL
	sliced green onion tops or chives	

1. Combine butter and leeks in an 8 cup (2 L) glass measure or micro-wavable casserole. Microwave, uncovered, at High (100%) for 2 to 4 minutes or until softened.

2. Stir mushrooms into leeks, coating well with butter. Microwave, uncovered, at High (100%) for 4 to 6 minutes or until tender, stirring once during cooking.

3. Blend in flour, salt and pepper and microwave, uncovered, at High (100%) for 1 minute. Gradually stir in Milk and chicken stock until smooth. Cover and microwave at High (100%) for 7 to 10 minutes, or until mixture comes to a boil and thickens. Stir twice during cooking. Add lemon juice or sherry.

4. Let stand, covered, for 5 minutes before serving. Season to taste with salt and pepper. Garnish with onion tops or chives.

Makes 5 cups (1.25 L).

CAULIFLOWER BISQUE WITH CHEESE CROUTONS

Cauliflower, with its high moisture content, microwaves easily to a tender state. For variety, try other vegetables such as broccoli, celery or squash.

1	medium cauliflower	1	
2 tbsp.	butter	30	mL
1	onion, chopped	1	
1	clove garlic, minced	1	
1 tbsp.	flour	15	mL
1/2 tsp.	dry mustard	2	mL
1/2 tsp.	salt	2	mL
1/4 tsp.	pepper	1	mL
1 cup	chicken stock or 1 tsp. (5 mL) chicken stock mix in 1 cup (250 mL) water	250	mL
2 cups	Milk	500	mL
Garnish			
2 tbsp.	butter	30	mL
2	slices bread, crusts removed and cubed	2	
1 tbsp.	grated Parmesan cheese	15	mL

1. Trim cauliflower into florets. Wash well and place in a large microwavable casserole. Cover and microwave at High (100%) for 8 to 10 minutes or until tender. Stir at least once during cooking. Let stand, covered, until needed.

2. Combine 2 tbsp. (30 mL) butter, onion and garlic in an 8 cup (2 L) glass measure or microwavable casserole. Microwave, uncovered, at High (100%) for 2 to 3 minutes or until softened.

3. Blend in flour, dry mustard, salt and pepper. Microwave, uncovered, at High (100%) for 30 seconds. Gradually stir in chicken stock until smooth. Cover and microwave at High (100%) for 3 to 5 minutes or until mixture comes to a boil and thickens slightly. Stir at least once during cooking.

4. Purée cauliflower in food processor or blender with sauce mixture until smooth. Return to dish and stir in Milk. Cover and microwave at High (100%) for 4 to 6 minutes or until heated through. Stir at least once during cooking.

5. Let stand, covered, for 5 minutes before serving. Season to taste with salt and pepper. If too thick, thin with a little extra Milk. Garnish each serving with cheese croutons.

Makes 6 cups (1.5 L)

Continued on next page

CAULIFLOWER BISQUE WITH CHEESE CROUTONS
(Continued)

To make croutons, melt 2 tbsp. (30 mL) butter in a shallow micro-wavable dish, such as a glass pie plate at High (100%) for 40 to 60 seconds. Toss bread cubes in butter, coating evenly. Sprinkle with cheese. Microwave, uncovered, at High (100%) for 3 to 4 minutes or until crisp. Stir or shake dish often. When cool, break up any that have stuck together. (Croutons will continue to crisp up during standing time.)

COLD CRAB SOUP

This chilled soup has a very subtle curry taste. If you prefer more, increase the curry powder.

2 tbsp.	butter	30 mL
1	leek, white part only, washed well and sliced	1
2 tbsp.	flour	30 mL
1/2 tsp.	curry powder	2 mL
2 cups	Milk	500 mL
1	4.23 oz. (120 g) can crab meat	1
2 tbsp.	dry white wine or vermouth	30 mL
1 tbsp.	lemon juice	15 mL
	salt and white pepper	
	chopped chives	

1. Combine butter and leek in an 8 cup (2 L) glass measure or micro-wavable casserole. Microwave, uncovered, at High (100%) for 2 to 3 minutes or until leek is softened.

2. Blend in flour and curry and microwave, uncovered, at High (100%) for 30 seconds. Gradually stir in Milk until smooth. Cover and microwave at High (100%) for 4 to 6 minutes or until mixture comes to a boil and thickens. Stir at least once during cooking.

3. Stir in crab meat, wine and lemon juice. Cover and chill well.

4. Before serving, season to taste with salt and pepper. Garnish with chives.

Makes 4 cups (1 L).

KETTLE OF FISH CHOWDER

Bacon and potato give this chunky soup a true chowder taste. The fish remains tender and moist when microwaved with the Milk.

3	slices bacon, diced	3
1	onion, chopped	1
1	stalk celery, chopped	1
2	medium potatoes, peeled and diced	2
1 cup	frozen peas	250 mL
1/2 tsp.	salt	2 mL
1/4 tsp.	pepper	1 mL
1 tsp.	Worcestershire sauce	5 mL
1 lb.	cod or halibut,* cut into 1 inch (2.5 cm) pieces	500 g
2 1/2 cups	Milk	625 mL
	chopped fresh parsley or paprika	

1. Combine bacon, onion and celery in an 8 cup (2 L) glass measure or microwavable casserole. Microwave, uncovered, at High (100%) for 3 to 4 minutes or until vegetables are softened.

2. Add potatoes and stir well to coat with mixture. Cover and microwave at High (100%) for 6 to 8 minutes or until potatoes are tender. Stir once during cooking.

3. Stir peas, salt, pepper and Worcestershire sauce into hot potato mixture. Add fish and Milk, cover and microwave at High (100%) for 10 to 14 minutes or until fish is cooked. Stir at least twice during cooking.

4. Let stand, covered, for 5 minutes before serving. Season to taste with salt and pepper. Garnish with parsley or paprika.

Makes 7 cups (1.75 L).

* If using frozen fish, cut it up without thawing and add 2 to 3 minutes to the cooking time.

CURRIED AVOCADO SOUP

Buy a very ripe avocado for maximum flavour—it will also purée easily. Unusual maybe, but the horseradish perks up the flavour in this cold soup.

2 tbsp.	butter	30	mL
1	onion, chopped	1	
1	stalk celery, chopped	1	
1	clove garlic, minced	1	
3 tbsp.	flour	45	mL
1 tsp.	curry powder	5	mL
1/2 tsp.	ground cumin	2	mL
1/2 tsp.	salt	2	mL
1/4 tsp.	pepper	1	mL
1 cup	chicken stock or 1 tsp. (5 mL) chicken stock mix in 1 cup (250 mL) water	250	mL
1	large, ripe avocado	1	
2 cups	Milk	500	mL
1 tbsp.	lemon juice	15	mL
2 tsp.	horseradish	10	mL
	sour cream		

1. Combine butter, onion, celery and garlic in an 8 cup (2 L) glass measure or microwavable casserole. Microwave, uncovered, at High (100%) for 2 to 3 minutes or until vegetables are softened.

2. Blend in flour, curry, cumin, salt and pepper and microwave, uncovered, at High (100%) for 30 seconds. Gradually stir in chicken stock until smooth. Cover and microwave at High (100%) for 3 to 5 minutes or until mixture comes to a boil and thickens. Stir at least once during cooking.

3. Peel and cube avocado. Place in food processor or blender along with stock mixture and purée until smooth. Return to dish and stir in Milk, lemon juice and horseradish. Cover and chill well.

4. Before serving, season to taste with salt and pepper. If necessary, thin with a little additional Milk. Stir well and garnish each serving with a swirl of sour cream.

Makes 5 cups (1.25 L).

ICED SPINACH SOUP

Colourful and cool, just right for those hot nights when you want to keep the kitchen and yourself cool. This green flecked soup is also good served hot.

1	10 oz. (300 g) package frozen, chopped spinach	1
2 tbsp.	butter	30 mL
1	onion, chopped	1
3 tbsp.	flour	45 mL
1/2 tsp.	salt	2 mL
1/2 tsp.	dry mustard	2 mL
1/4 tsp.	pepper	1 mL
1 cup	chicken stock or 1 tsp. chicken stock mix in 1 cup (250 mL) water	250 mL
1/2 tsp.	dried dill weed or 1 tbsp. (15 mL) chopped fresh dill	2 mL
1/2 tsp.	sugar	2 mL
2 cups	Milk	500 mL
	lemon peel	

1. Remove spinach from package and place on a microwavable plate. Cover with vented plastic wrap and microwave at High (100%) for 3 to 4 minutes or until thawed. Break up with a fork partway through cooking. Drain well and purée in food processor or blender.

2. Combine butter and onion in an 8 cup (2 L) glass measure or micro-wavable casserole. Microwave, uncovered, at High (100%) for 2 to 3 minutes or until softened.

3. Blend in flour, salt, mustard and pepper and microwave, uncovered, at High (100%) for 30 seconds. Gradually stir in chicken stock until smooth. Cover and microwave at High (100%) for 3 to 5 minutes or until mixture comes to a boil and thickens. Stir at least once during cooking. Stir in dill weed and sugar.

4. Add to spinach in food processor or blender and purée until smooth. Return to dish and stir in Milk until smooth. If serving cold, cover and chill well. Before serving, season to taste with salt and pepper, and thin if necessary with a little Milk. Garnish each serving with a strip of lemon peel.

5. If serving hot, cover and microwave at High (100%) for 4 to 6 minutes or until heated through. Stir at least once during cooking. Let stand, covered, for 5 minutes before serving. Season to taste with salt and pepper. Garnish, if desired, with lemon peel.

Makes 4 cups (1 L).

CHILLED VICHYSSOISE SUPREME

This traditional potato and leek soup is good served either cold or hot. It will thicken when chilled, so you may wish to thin with additional Milk.

2 tbsp.	butter	30 mL
3	leeks, white part only, washed well and sliced	3
1 lb.	potatoes, peeled and diced (about 3 medium)	500 g
1 cup	chicken broth or 1 tsp. (5 mL) chicken stock mix in 1 cup (250 mL) water	250 mL
2 cups	Milk	500 mL
	salt and pepper	
	chopped chives	

1. Combine butter, leeks and potatoes in an 8 cup (2 L) glass measure or microwavable casserole. Cover and microwave at High (100%) for 6 to 8 minutes or until potatoes are almost tender. Stir at least once during cooking.

2. Stir in chicken broth, cover and microwave for 4 to 6 minutes or until potatoes are tender. Let stand, covered, for 5 minutes.

3. Purée in food processor or blender until smooth. Return to dish and stir in Milk. If serving cold, cover and chill well. If serving hot, cover and microwave at High (100%) for 4 to 6 minutes or until heated through.

4. Let stand, covered, for 5 minutes. Season to taste with salt and pepper. Garnish with chopped chives.

Makes 5 cups (1.25 L).

CLASSIC WHITE SAUCE

This classic easy-to-make Milk sauce is even easier in the microwave. No scorching or messy pots to clean. To the basic sauce a number of flavours can be added. Try Cheese Sauce over green vegetables or cauliflower, Mustard Sauce with braised celery or ham and Summer Sauce on new potatoes.

THIN	1 tbsp.	butter	15	mL
	1 tbsp.	flour	15	mL
	1/4 tsp.	salt	1	mL
	1 cup	Milk	250	mL
MEDIUM	2 tbsp.	butter	30	mL
	2 tbsp.	flour	30	mL
	1/4 tsp.	salt	1	mL
	1 cup	Milk	250	mL
THICK	3 tbsp.	butter	45	mL
	3 tbsp.	flour	45	mL
	1/4 tsp.	salt	1	mL
	1 cup	Milk	250	mL

1. Melt butter in a 4 cup (1 L) glass measure at High (100%) for 30 to 60 seconds. Blend in flour and salt to make a smooth paste. Microwave, uncovered, at High (100%) for 30 seconds.

2. Gradually whisk in Milk until smooth. Microwave, uncovered, at High (100%) for 3 to 5 minutes, or until sauce comes to a boil and thickens. Whisk partway through cooking.

Makes 1 cup (250 mL).

SAVOURY SAUCES

Cheese Sauce: Stir 1/2 to 1 cup (125 to 250 mL) shredded cheese into warm sauce until melted. If necessary, microwave at Medium (50%) for 30 to 60 seconds to help melt cheese.

Mustard Sauce: Blend 1 tbsp. (15 mL) prepared mustard into sauce.

Summer Sauce: Stir 1 tbsp. (15 mL) each of chopped fresh parsley and green onions or chives into sauce.

Dill Sauce: Stir 1 tsp.(5 mL) lemon juice, then 1 tbsp. (15 mL) chopped fresh dill into warm sauce. Serve with fish or shellfish.

Horseradish Sauce: Add 1 to 2 tbsp. (15 to 30 mL) horseradish to warm white sauce. Excellent with beef or veal.

CHEDDAR SAUCE SUPREME

A tasty sauce to toss over cooked pasta, vegetables or toast or to use as a speedy fondue.

2 tbsp.	butter	30 mL
3 tbsp.	flour	45 mL
1 tsp.	chicken stock mix or 1 chicken bouillon cube, crushed	5 mL
pinch	dry mustard	pinch
1 1/2 cups	Milk	375 mL
1 1/2 cups	shredded Cheddar cheese salt and pepper	375 mL

1. Melt butter in a 4 cup (1 L) glass measure at High (100%) for 30 to 45 seconds. Blend in flour, stock mix and dry mustard. Microwave, uncovered, at High (100%) for 30 seconds.

2. Gradually whisk in Milk until smooth. Microwave, uncovered, at High (100%) for 4 to 6 minutes or until sauce comes to a boil and thickens. Whisk at least once during cooking.

3. Stir in cheese until melted. If necessary, microwave at Medium (50%) for 30 to 60 seconds to help melt cheese. Season to taste with salt and pepper.

Makes 2 cups (500 mL).

VARIATION:

Mornay Sauce: Replace Cheddar cheese with Swiss cheese and serve with fish, shellfish or vegetables.

SAVOURY MUSHROOM SAUCE

A different sauce for cannelloni or lasagna instead of the usual tomato sauce.

2 tbsp.	butter	30 mL
3 cups	sliced fresh mushrooms	750 mL
1	small onion, chopped	1
1/4 cup	flour	50 mL
1 tsp.	chicken stock mix or 1 chicken bouillon cube, crushed	5 mL
1 1/2 cups	Milk salt and pepper	375 mL

1. Combine butter, mushrooms and onion in an 8 cup (2 L) glass measure. Microwave, uncovered, at High (100%) for 3 to 4 minutes, or until vegetables are tender. Stir partway through cooking. Blend in flour and stock mix. Microwave, uncovered, at High (100%) for 30 seconds.

2. Gradually stir in Milk until smooth. Microwave, uncovered, at High (100%) for 5 to 7 minutes or until sauce comes to a boil and thickens. Stir at least once during cooking. Season to taste with salt and pepper. Thin, if necessary, with a little extra Milk.

Makes 3 cups (750 mL).

VARIATION:

Creamy Onion Sauce: Omit mushrooms and add an additional chopped onion. Serve with vegetables, meat, fish or pasta.

SMOKE HOUSE BACON SAUCE

For a little different breakfast or brunch, spoon sauce over hard cooked or poached eggs on toast.

4	slices bacon, diced	4	
1	small onion, chopped	1	
2 tbsp.	flour	30	mL
1 1/2 cups	Milk	375	mL
1/2 cup	grated Parmesan cheese	125	mL
2 tbsp.	chopped fresh parsley	30	mL
	salt and pepper		

1. Combine bacon and onion in a 4 cup (1 L) glass measure. Microwave, uncovered, at High (100%) for 3 to 4 minutes, or until onion is tender and bacon is cooked. Stir partway through cooking. Blend in flour and microwave, uncovered, at High (100%) for 30 seconds.

2. Gradually whisk in Milk until smooth. Microwave, uncovered, at High (100%) for 4 to 6 minutes or until sauce comes to a boil and thickens. Whisk at least once during cooking. Stir in cheese until melted. Add parsley and season to taste with salt and pepper.

Makes 2 cups (500 mL).

CURRY SAUCE

When you have leftover cooked chicken, turkey or roast, keep this versatile sauce in mind for a quick meal. Cut meat into cubes and add to cooked sauce. Serve over rice or noodles.

2 tbsp.	butter	30	mL
1	small onion, chopped	1	
1	small stalk celery, chopped or 1/2 cup (125 mL) chopped green or red pepper	1	
3 tbsp.	flour	45	mL
1-2 tsp.	curry powder	5-10	mL
1 tsp.	chicken stock mix or 1 chicken bouillon cube, crushed	5	mL
1 1/2 cups	Milk	375	mL
	salt and pepper		

1. Combine butter, onion and celery or pepper in an 4 cup (1 L) glass measure. Microwave, uncovered, at High (100%) for 2 to 4 minutes, or until vegetables are softened. Stir partway through cooking. Blend in flour, curry powder and stock mix. Microwave, uncovered, at High (100%) for 30 seconds.

2. Gradually whisk in Milk until smooth. Microwave, uncovered, at High (100%) for 4 to 6 minutes or until sauce comes to a boil and thickens. Whisk at least once during cooking. Season to taste with salt and pepper.

Makes 2 cups (500 mL).

QUICK AND EASY DESSERT SAUCES

What could be simpler than a creamy vanilla sauce from a pudding mix. Serve with fresh fruit.

1	package (4 serving size) vanilla pudding and pie filling	1
3 cups	Milk	750 mL
2 tsp.	vanilla	10 mL

1. Combine pudding mix and Milk in an 8 cup (2 L) glass measure. Microwave, uncovered, at High (100%) for 9 to 12 minutes or until mixture comes to a boil and thickens. Whisk 3 or 4 times during cooking. Add vanilla.

2. To prevent a skin from forming, place plastic wrap directly on surface of sauce. Cool, then chill. Store covered in refrigerator for up to 1 week.

Makes 3 1/2 cups (875 mL).

VARIATIONS:

Café au Lait Sauce: Add 2 tbsp. (30 mL) instant coffee granules with Milk. Add sugar to taste and cook as above. Serve with slices of chocolate cake.

Orange Sauce: Add 1 tbsp. (15 mL) grated orange peel with Milk. Cook as above. Reduce vanilla to 1 tsp. (5 mL).

REGAL CHOCOLATE SAUCE

A rich and indulgent chocolate sauce to pour over ice cream. A number of flavourful additions make for delicious variations.

1	12 oz. (350 g) package semi-sweet chocolate pieces	1
1/3 cup	butter	75 mL
3 tbsp.	corn syrup	45 mL
1 cup	Milk	250 mL
1 tsp.	vanilla	5 mL

1. Combine chocolate, butter, corn syrup and Milk in a 4 cup (1 L) glass measure. Microwave, uncovered, at High (100%) for 3 to 5 minutes or until butter and chocolate melt. Stir at least once during cooking to help the melting. Stir in vanilla.

2. Cool to room temperature. Sauce will thicken as it cools. Serve over ice cream. Store leftover sauce in a covered jar in refrigerator. Reheat as necessary.

Makes 2 1/2 cups (625 mL).

VARIATIONS:

Mocha Sauce: Stir 1 tbsp. (15 mL) instant coffee granules into warm sauce until dissolved.

Chocolate Orange Sauce: Stir 2 tbsp. (30 mL) orange liqueur into warm sauce.

Chocolate Almond Sauce: Add 1 1/2 tsp. (7 mL) almond extract and 1 tbsp. (15 mL) almond liqueur to warm sauce.

Chocolate Mint Sauce: Add 1 to 1 1/2 tsp. (5 to 7 mL) peppermint extract to sauce.

Chocolate Rum Sauce: Stir 1 1/2 tsp. (7 mL) rum extract to warm sauce.

CREAMY LEMON SAUCE

A wonderful sauce to dress up a plain cake, gingerbread or to pour over ice cream.

1/2 cup	sugar	125 mL
2 tbsp.	cornstarch	30 mL
1 1/4 cups	Milk	300 mL
2 tbsp.	butter	30 mL
1 tsp.	grated lemon peel	5 mL
3 tbsp.	lemon juice	45 mL

1. Combine sugar and cornstarch in a 4 cup (1 L) glass measure. Whisk in Milk until smooth. Microwave, uncovered, at High (100%) for 3 to 5 minutes or until sauce comes to a boil and thickens. Whisk partway through cooking.

2. Stir in butter until melted, then stir in lemon peel and juice. Serve warm. Store any leftover sauce in refrigerator.

Makes 1 3/4 cups (425 mL).

VARIATION:

Creamy Orange Sauce: Substitute orange peel and juice for the lemon.

CUSTARD SAUCE

This traditional English sauce is a breeze to make in the microwave. Eggs both thicken and flavour this classic sauce. Serve with steamed puddings, pies or in trifles.

1/4 cup	sugar	50 mL
2 tbsp.	cornstarch	30 mL
1 1/2 cups	Milk	375 mL
2	eggs, lightly beaten	2
1 tsp.	vanilla	5 mL
1 tsp.	grated lemon peel, optional	5 mL

1. Combine sugar and cornstarch in a 4 cup (1 L) glass measure. Whisk in Milk until smooth. Microwave, uncovered, at High (100%) for 4 to 6 minutes or until sauce comes to a boil and thickens. Whisk twice during cooking.

2. Stir a small amount of hot sauce into lightly beaten eggs. Pour warmed eggs back into sauce, whisking constantly.

3. Microwave, uncovered, at Medium (50%) for 1 minute. Stir in vanilla and lemon peel, if using.

4. To prevent a skin from forming, cover surface of warm sauce with plastic wrap.

Makes 2 cups (500 mL).

MAIN COURSES

Beef and Pasta Supper

Baked Fish Creole

Main Courses

Milk, meat and the microwave have teamed up to make some delicious dishes—spicy meatloaf, fish baked Creole-style, and a kids' favourite, Cheeseburger Pie. The need for fast dinners has been met with recipes using cooked ham, chicken and turkey, a quick cooking Moussaka and a tasty fish dish baked with aromatic herbs.

Lower power levels such as Medium-High (70%) for chicken and Medium (50%) for cubes or strips of beef or pork, provide gentle and even cooking without toughening. With meat, it's best to use shorter cooking times and check often to avoid overcooking.

CREOLE MEATLOAF

A ring or donut shape is the ideal cooking shape for microwave meatloaves.

3 tbsp.	butter	45 mL
1	onion, chopped	1
2	cloves garlic, minced	2
1	green pepper, finely chopped	1
1	red pepper, finely chopped	1
3 tbsp.	flour	45 mL
1 1/2 cups	Milk	375 mL
1/3 cup	chili sauce or ketchup	75 mL
2 tbsp.	tomato paste	30 mL
1 tsp.	salt	5 mL
1/4 tsp.	cayenne or Tabasco sauce	1 mL
1/4 tsp.	pepper	1 mL
1 tsp.	Worcestershire sauce	5 mL
1 1/2 lbs.	lean ground beef	750 g
1	egg	1
1/2 cup	dry breadcrumbs	125 mL
1/2 tsp.	salt	2 mL

1. Combine butter, onion, garlic, green and red peppers in an 8 cup (2 L) glass measure. Microwave, uncovered, at High (100%) for 4 to 5 minutes or until vegetables are softened.

2. Blend in flour and microwave at High (100%) for 1 minute. Gradually whisk in Milk until smooth. Cover and microwave at High (100%) for 4 to 6 minutes or until mixture comes to a boil and thickens. Whisk at least once during cooking.

3. Add chili sauce, tomato paste, 1 tsp. (5 mL) salt, cayenne, pepper and Worcestershire sauce. Cover and microwave at High (100%) for 3 to 5 minutes or until hot. Stir at least once during cooking. Season to taste with salt and pepper. Cool.

4. Combine meat with egg, breadcrumbs, 1/2 tsp. (2 mL) salt and 1/2 cup (125 mL) of sauce. Lightly pack into a 6 cup (1.5 L) microwave ring mould. If you do not have a microwavable ring mould, place a small custard cup in the centre of a round 8 cup (2 L) microwavable casserole or shape into an 8 inch (20 cm) ring shape on a large glass pie plate. Pour remaining sauce on top of loaf.

5. Microwave, uncovered, at High (100%) for 18 to 24 minutes. Rotate dish, if necessary, once or twice during cooking. Drain off excess fat and let stand 5 to 10 minutes before serving. Slice to serve.

Serves 4-6

BEEF AND PASTA SUPPER

This is a colourful, one-dish dinner. Serve with a salad and crusty bread.

1 lb.	lean ground beef	500	g
2 cups	sliced fresh mushrooms	500	mL
1	large onion, chopped	1	
1	green pepper, chopped	1	
2	cloves garlic, minced	2	
3 tbsp.	flour	45	mL
1-2 tbsp.	taco seasoning mix	15-30	mL
1 1/2 cups	Milk	375	mL
1	28 oz.(796 mL) can tomatoes, undrained	1	
3/4 cup	elbow macaroni salt and pepper	175	mL

1. Crumble ground beef in a 12 cup (3 L) microwavable casserole. Add mushrooms, onion, green pepper and garlic. Microwave, uncovered, at High (100%) for 5 to 7 minutes or until beef is no longer pink and vegetables are softened. Stir 2 or 3 times during cooking to break up meat. Drain off fat.

2. Blend flour and taco seasoning into meat mixture. Microwave, uncovered, at High (100%) for 1 minute. Gradually stir in Milk until smooth. Cover and microwave at High (100%) for 4 to 6 minutes or until mixture comes to a boil and thickens. Stir once or twice.

3. Add tomatoes, along with juice and pasta. Mash tomatoes with a potato masher or fork. Cover and microwave at Medium (50%) for 18 to 20 minutes or until pasta is tender. Stir 3 times during cooking.

4. Let stand, covered, for a few minutes before serving. Season to taste with salt and pepper.

Serves 4 to 6.

SHEPHERD'S PIE WITH CHEESY MASHED POTATOES

A traditional favourite that's been updated for the microwave.

2 lbs.	potatoes, peeled and quartered	1	kg
1/3 cup	water	75	mL
3/4 cup	Milk	175	mL
2 tbsp.	butter	30	mL
3/4 cup	shredded Cheddar cheese	175	mL
	salt and pepper		
2 lbs.	lean ground beef	1	kg
2	onions, chopped	2	
2	cloves garlic, minced	2	
2 tbsp.	flour	30	mL
1 cup	Milk	250	mL
1	19 oz. (540 mL) can tomatoes, drained	1	
1/4 tsp.	Tabasco sauce	1	mL
1 tsp.	Worcestershire sauce	5	mL
1/2 tsp.	dried thyme	2	mL
3/4 cup	fresh breadcrumbs	175	mL
1/2 cup	frozen peas	125	mL
1 tsp.	paprika	5	mL

1. Combine potatoes and water in an 8 cup (2 L) microwavable casserole. Cover and microwave at High (100%) for 12 to 18 minutes or until tender. Stir once or twice during cooking. Let stand, covered, for 5 minutes.

2. Microwave the 3/4 cup (175 mL) Milk in a 1 cup (250 mL) glass measure at High (100%) for 1-1/2 to 2 minutes or until hot. Drain potatoes and mash with hot Milk, butter, and cheese. Add salt and pepper to taste. Set aside.

3. Crumble ground beef, onions and garlic into a 12 cup (3 L) microwavable casserole. Microwave, uncovered, at High (100%) for 5 to 8 minutes or until meat loses its pink colour. Stir often to break up lumps. Drain off fat.

4. Stir in flour and microwave at High (100%) for 30 seconds. Stir in the 1 cup (250 mL) Milk and tomatoes, mashing with a potato masher or fork. Cover and microwave at High (100%) for 5 to 8 minutes or until slightly thickened. Stir twice during cooking. Stir in seasonings, breadcrumbs and peas. Season to taste with salt and pepper.

Continued on next page

SHEPHERD'S PIE WITH
CHEESY MASHED POTATOES

(Continued)

5. Spread or pipe mashed potatoes on top of meat mixture. Sprinkle lightly with paprika and microwave, uncovered, at Medium-High (70%) for 8 to 10 minutes or until heated through. Rotate dish, if necessary, during cooking. Let stand for 5 minutes before serving.

Serves 6.

BRAISED MEATBALLS IN MUSHROOM SAUCE

On a microwave rack, the meatballs not only retain their shape but brown quite nicely. These are then simmered in a creamy mushroom sauce.

1 lb.	lean ground beef	500	g
1/2 cup	breadcrumbs	125	mL
1/2 cup	Milk	125	mL
1/2 tsp.	salt	2	mL
1/4 tsp.	pepper	1	mL
1/4 tsp.	dried basil	1	mL
1/4 tsp.	dried oregano	1	mL
1	clove garlic, minced	1	
Sauce			
2 tbsp.	butter	30	mL
1	onion, chopped	1	
2 cups	sliced mushrocms	500	mL
1/4 cup	flour	50	mL
2 cups	Milk	500	mL
2 tsp.	Worcestershire sauce	10	mL
2 tsp.	soy sauce	10	mL
2 tsp.	Dijon mustard	10	mL
1/4 tsp.	salt	1	mL
1/4 tsp.	pepper	1	mL
2 tbsp.	chopped fresh parsley	30	mL

1. Combine beef, breadcrumbs, Milk, 1/2 tsp. (2 mL) salt, 1/4 tsp. (1 mL) pepper, basil, oregano and garlic. Mix well and shape into 1 1/2 inch (4 cm) meatballs (16 to 20).

2. Arrange meatballs evenly on a microwave roasting rack about 1/2 inch (1 cm) apart. Cover with waxed paper and microwave at High (100%) for 5 to 7 minutes or until no longer pink in centre. Rotate rack or rearrange meatballs, as necessary, during cooking. It may be necessary to do this in two batches to allow for even cooking. If so, divide cooking time accordingly. Let stand, covered, while making sauce.

3. Combine butter, onion and mushrooms in a 12 cup (3 L) microwavable casserole. Microwave, uncovered, at High (100%) for 4 to 6 minutes or until mushrooms are tender. Stir at least once during cooking.

Continued on next page

BRAISED MEATBALLS IN MUSHROOM SAUCE
(Continued)

4. Blend in flour and microwave at High (100%) for 1 minute. Gradually stir in Milk until smooth. Cover and microwave at High (100%) for 6 to 8 minutes or until mixture comes to a boil and thickens.

5. Add Worcestershire sauce, soy sauce, mustard, 1/4 tsp. (1 mL) salt and 1/4 tsp. (1 mL) pepper. Stir in meatballs, cover and microwave at High (100%) for 2 to 4 minutes or until heated through. Season to taste with salt and pepper. Sprinkle with parsley and serve over rice or noodles.

Serves 4 to 6.

BEEF AND CHEESE ENCHILADAS

Purchased taco sauce simplifies these enchiladas. Buy mild, medium or hot depending on your preference.

1/2 lb.	lean ground beef	250	g
1	onion, chopped	1	
1	clove garlic, minced	1	
1/2 cup	chopped green pepper	125	mL
1 tbsp.	chili powder	15	mL
2 tsp.	flour	10	mL
1 tsp.	ground cumin	5	mL
1	8 oz. (227 mL) jar or can taco sauce (mild, medium or hot)	1	
2 tbsp.	butter	30	mL
2 tbsp.	flour	30	mL
3/4 cup	Milk	175	mL
3/4 cup	shredded Cheddar cheese	175	mL
4	8 inch (20 cm) flour tortillas	4	

1. Crumble ground beef into a 6 cup (1.5 L) microwavable casserole. Add onion, garlic and green pepper and microwave, uncovered, at High (100%) for 2 to 4 minutes or until meat is no longer pink. Stir twice to break up lumps.

2. Stir chili powder, 2 tsp. (10 mL) flour and cumin into mixture and microwave, uncovered, at High (100%) for 1 minute. Stir 1/2 cup (125 mL) of the taco sauce into beef mixture. Cover and microwave at High (100%) for 2 to 4 minutes or until mixture comes to a boil and thickens. Stir at least once during cooking. Let stand, covered, while making sauce.

3. Melt butter in a 4 cup (1 L) glass measure at High (100%) for 30 to 50 seconds. Blend in 2 tbsp. (30 mL) flour and microwave at High (100%) for 30 seconds. Gradually stir in Milk and remaining taco sauce until smooth. Microwave, uncovered, at High (100%) for 2 to 4 minutes or until mixture comes to a boil and thickens. Stir at least once during cooking.

4. Spoon 1/4 of beef mixture down centre of each tortilla. Sprinkle each with 2 tbsp. (30 mL) cheese. Fold edges over and place seam side down in a shallow microwavable dish such as an 11 x 7 inch (2 L). Pour sauce down centre of enchiladas and sprinkle remaining cheese over sauce. Cover with waxed paper and microwave at Medium-High (70%) for 2 to 4 minutes or until heated through.

Serves 4.

MEXICAN BEEF AND BEAN CASSEROLE

A cornmeal base and a zesty, colourful beef, bean and corn mixture make up this hearty casserole.

3/4 cup	cornmeal	175 mL
2 cups	Milk	500 mL
1/2 tsp.	salt	2 mL
1 cup	shredded Cheddar cheese, divided	250 mL
1/2 lb.	lean ground beef	250 g
1	onion, chopped	1
1	clove garlic, minced	1
1/2 cup	chopped green pepper	125 mL
1 tsp.	ground cumin	5 mL
pinch	cayenne	pinch
1	14 oz. (398 mL) can kidney beans and liquid	1
1	12 oz. (341 mL) can whole kernel corn, drained	1
	salt, pepper and Tabasco sauce	

1. Combine cornmeal, Milk and salt in a 12 cup (3 L) microwavable casserole. Stir well, cover and microwave at High (100%) for 6 to 8 minutes or until liquid is absorbed. Stir partway through cooking and at the end. Stir in 1/2 cup (125 mL) of the cheese until melted. Smooth mixture in bottom of casserole. Let stand, covered, while making beef mixture.

2. Crumble ground beef into an 8 cup (2 L) microwavable casserole. Add onion, garlic and green pepper and microwave, uncovered, at High (100%) for 3 to 5 minutes or until meat is no longer pink. Stir twice to break up lumps. Pour off fat.

3. Stir cumin and cayenne into beef mixture. Add kidney beans and corn. Cover and microwave at High (100%) for 4 to 6 minutes or until heated through. Stir at least once during cooking. Season to taste with salt, pepper and Tabasco.

4. Spoon over cornmeal base, then sprinkle with remaining 1/2 cup (125 mL) cheese. Cover and let stand a few minutes to melt cheese.

Serves 4 to 6.

CHEESEBURGER PIE

If it's the kids' turn to cook, this is the one to make. It's simple and can be made in record time.

1 lb.	lean ground beef	500	g
1 cup	Milk, divided	250	mL
1/2 cup	dry breadcrumbs	125	mL
1 tsp.	Worcestershire sauce	5	mL
1/2 tsp.	dried basil	2	mL
1/4 tsp.	salt	1	mL
1/4 tsp.	pepper	1	mL
1 tbsp.	butter	15	mL
1 tbsp.	flour	15	mL
1 cup	shredded Cheddar cheese, divided	250	mL
1	medium ripe tomato, sliced thinly	1	

1. Combine beef, Milk, breadcrumbs, Worcestershire sauce, basil, salt and pepper. Press into a 9 inch (23 cm) glass pie plate to make a crust, building up sides. Cover with waxed paper and microwave at High (100%) for 5 to 7 minutes or until meat is no longer pink. Rotate dish, if necessary, partway through cooking. Drain off fat and let stand, covered, while making sauce.

2. Melt butter in a 4 cup (1 L) glass measure at High (100%) for 20 to 40 seconds. Blend in flour and microwave, uncovered, at High (100%) for 20 seconds. Gradually stir in 1/2 cup (125 mL) of the Milk until smooth. Microwave, uncovered, at High (100%) for 1 1/2 to 3 minutes or until mixture comes to a boil and thickens. Stir at least once during cooking. Stir in 3/4 cup (175 mL) of the cheese until melted.

3. Pour off any accumulated juices on meat crust. Spread tomato slices evenly over crust, then pour cheese sauce over all. Sprinkle with remaining cheese. Let stand a few minutes to melt cheese. Cut into wedges and serve.

Serves 4.

PORK CHOPS WITH APPLES AND RAISINS

Serve this delicious cool weather combination over buttered noodles or rice.

2 tbsp.	butter	30	mL
1	onion, chopped	1	
1	clove garlic, minced	1	
1 tsp.	beef stock mix	5	mL
1/2 tsp.	dried thyme	2	mL
1/2 cup	frozen apple juice concentrate, thawed	125	mL
6	loin pork chops, about 1/2 inch (1 cm) thick	6	
2	large apples, cored and sliced crosswise into 1/2 inch (1 cm) slices	2	
1/4 cup	raisins	50	mL
1 1/3 cups	Milk	325	mL
3 tbsp.	flour	45	mL
	salt and pepper		

1. Combine butter, onion and garlic in a shallow microwavable dish that holds the pork chops in a single layer. Cover with vented plastic wrap and microwave at High (100%) for 2 to 3 minutes or until softened. Stir in beef stock mix, thyme and apple juice concentrate. Arrange pork chops over onions with meaty portions towards outer edges of dish. Top with apple slices and raisins.

2. Re-cover and microwave at Medium (50%) for 25 to 30 minutes or until meat next to bone is no longer pink when cut. Turn chops over and rearrange partway through cooking. (This lower power level, (50%), helps to ensure tender chops.) Turn over and rearrange as necessary for even cooking.

3. Transfer chops and apples to serving platter, cover and keep warm. Combine Milk and flour until smooth. Stir into liquid in dish. Microwave, uncovered, at High (100%) for 8 to 10 minutes or until mixture boils and thickens. Stir 3 or 4 times during cooking. Season to taste with salt and pepper.

4. To serve, pour sauce over chops and apples.

Serves 6.

PORK PASTITSIO

This is a popular layered Greek casserole of macaroni, a meat-tomato mixture and a cheese sauce. The eggs in the dish allow it to "set", so do not stir during final cooking and give it a good standing time.

1 1/2 cups	macaroni	375	mL
1/2 cup	shredded Cheddar cheese	125	mL
1	egg, lightly beaten	1	
1 lb.	ground pork	500	g
1	onion, chopped	1	
1	clove garlic, minced	1	
1/2 tsp.	salt	2	mL
1/2 tsp.	dried oregano	2	mL
1/4 tsp.	cinnamon	1	mL
1/4 tsp.	pepper	1	mL
1	7 1/2 oz. (213 mL) can tomato sauce	1	
Sauce			
2 tbsp.	butter	30	mL
2 tbsp.	flour	30	mL
1 cup	Milk	250	mL
1 cup	shredded Cheddar cheese	250	mL
1	egg, lightly beaten	1	

1. Cook macaroni conventionally according to package directions until al dente (tender but firm). Rinse briefly under cold water. Drain well and mix with the 1/2 cup (125 mL) cheese and egg. Spread half in the bottom of a round 8 cup (2 L) microwavable casserole.

2. While macaroni is cooking, crumble pork in another 8 cup (2 L) micro-wavable casserole. Add onion and garlic and microwave, uncovered, at High (100%) for 5 to 7 minutes or until pork is no longer pink. Stir often to break up lumps. Drain off fat.

3. Season meat with salt, oregano, cinnamon and pepper. Stir in tomato sauce, cover and microwave at High (100%) for 2 to 4 minutes or until mixture comes to a boil. Stir at least once during cooking. Top macaroni layer with meat mixture, then cover with remaining macaroni.

4. Melt butter in a 4 cup (1 L) glass measure for 30 to 50 seconds. Blend in flour and microwave at High (100%) for 30 seconds. Gradually whisk in Milk until smooth. Microwave, uncovered, at High (100%) for 3 to 5 minutes or until mixture comes to a boil and thickens. Whisk at least twice during cooking. Stir in cheese until melted, then stir in lightly beaten egg, mixing well.

Continued on next page

PORK PASTITSIO

(Continued)

5. Pour sauce over macaroni and meat layers. Cover and microwave at Medium-High (70%) for 6 to 8 minutes or until heated through and set. Rotate, as necessary, but do not stir. Let stand, covered, for 15 minutes before serving.

Serves 6.

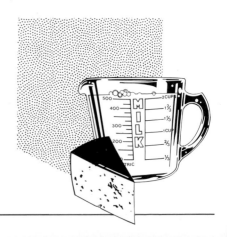

PORK 'N' PINEAPPLE

A quick sauté on top of the stove will give these tender pieces an attractive colour. Do not overcook the pork in the microwave or it will toughen. Serve over cooked rice or noodles.

2 tbsp.	butter	30	mL
1 lb.	pork tenderloin, cut into 1/2 inch (1 cm) slices	500	g
1 tbsp.	butter	15	mL
1	red or green pepper, thinly sliced	1	
6	green onions, diagonally sliced	6	
1	clove garlic, minced	1	
1 tbsp.	flour	15	mL
1/2 tsp.	ground ginger	2	mL
1/2 tsp.	curry powder	2	mL
1/2 tsp.	ground cumin	2	mL
1/4 tsp.	salt	1	mL
1/4 tsp.	pepper	1	mL
1 cup	Milk	250	mL
1 cup	well drained pineapple chunks salt and pepper	250	mL

1. Heat 2 tbsp. (30 mL) butter in a large skillet on stove top. Quickly sauté pork slices a few at a time over high heat, just until browned on both sides. Remove with tongs or a slotted spoon and set aside. Continue until all are browned.

2. Combine 1 tbsp. (15 mL) butter, red pepper, green onions and garlic in an 8 cup (2 L) microwavable casserole. Microwave, uncovered, at High (100%) for 2 to 4 minutes or until pepper is softened.

3. Blend in flour, ginger, curry, cumin, salt and pepper. Microwave, uncovered, at High (100%) for 30 seconds. Gradually stir in Milk until smooth. Cover and microwave at High (100%) for 3 to 5 minutes or until slightly thickened. Stir twice during cooking.

4. Stir in pork slices, cover and microwave at High (100%) for 4 minutes, then at Medium (50%) for 5 to 10 minutes or until pork is tender and no longer pink in the centre. Stir twice during cooking.

5. Stir in pineapple chunks and let stand, covered, for 5 minutes before serving. Season to taste with salt and pepper.

Serves 4.

MAPLE GLAZED HAM WITH MUSTARD SAUCE

Combination cooking at its best—broil ham steaks conventionally while making the sauce in the microwave. If you don't have Russian style mustard, use 1 tbsp. (15 mL) each of honey and Dijon mustard.

4	cooked packaged ham steaks, about 6 oz. (175 g) each	4
1/3 cup	maple syrup	75 mL
1 tbsp.	Dijon mustard	15 mL
3 tbsp.	butter	45 mL
3 tbsp.	flour	45 mL
2 cups	Milk	500 mL
1/4 tsp.	Tabasco sauce	1 mL
1 tbsp.	tomato paste	15 mL
1 tbsp.	Worcestershire sauce	15 mL
2 tbsp.	Russian style mustard salt and pepper paprika	30 mL

1. Preheat broiler. Line baking sheet with foil. Arrange ham steaks on a rack set over baking sheet. Combine maple syrup and mustard and brush over ham steaks. Broil until glazed, about 5 to 10 minutes, turning once and basting.

2. Meanwhile, melt butter in 4 cup (1 L) glass measure at High (100%) for 30 to 50 seconds. Blend in flour and microwave, uncovered, at High (100%) for 30 seconds. Gradually whisk in Milk until smooth. Microwave, uncovered, at High (100%) for 4 to 6 minutes or until sauce comes to a boil and thickens. Whisk twice during cooking. Add Tabasco, tomato paste, Worcestershire sauce and mustard. Season with salt and pepper to taste.

3. To serve, spoon sauce over ham and dust lightly with paprika.

Serves 4.

COUNTRY HAM CASSEROLE

This really is a "what's in the cupboard or fridge" casserole. Substitute different pasta shapes or soups, depending on what you have on hand.

2 cups	dried rotini, fusilli or cut ziti pasta	500 mL
2 tbsp.	butter	30 mL
1	onion, chopped	1
1/2 cup	chopped green or red pepper	125 mL
2 cups	cubed, cooked ham	500 mL
1 cup	shredded mozzarella cheese	250 mL
1	10 oz. (284 mL) can cream of celery or cream of mushroom soup	1
3/4 cup	Milk	175 mL
1 tbsp.	Dijon, Russian style or hot mustard salt and pepper	15 mL
1 tbsp.	grated Parmesan cheese	15 mL
1 tbsp.	chopped fresh parsley	15 mL

1. Cook pasta conventionally according to package directions until al dente (tender but firm). Drain.

2. While pasta is cooking, combine butter, onion and green pepper in a 12 cup (3 L) microwavable casserole. Microwave, uncovered, at High (100%) for 3 to 4 minutes or until vegetables are tender. Stir in ham, mozzarella cheese and pasta until well combined.

3. Blend soup, Milk and mustard together and pour over ham mixture. Stir well and season to taste with salt and pepper. Cover and microwave at Medium-High (70%) for 6 to 8 minutes or until heated through and cheese is melted. Stir once or twice during cooking.

4. Sprinkle with Parmesan cheese and parsley. Let stand, covered, for 5 to 10 minutes before serving.

Serves 4.

HAM ON ENGLISH MUFFINS

This quick, light supper dish is a wonderful way to serve the leftovers from an Easter ham.

2 tbsp.	butter	30 mL
1/4 cup	chopped green or red pepper	50 mL
2 tbsp.	flour	30 mL
1 tsp.	dry mustard	5 mL
	salt and pepper	
1 1/4 cups	Milk	300 mL
1 1/2 cups	cubed cooked ham	375 mL
1/4 cup	sour cream	50 mL
	salt and pepper	
4	English muffins, split and toasted	4

1. Combine butter and green pepper in a 4 cup (1 L) glass measure and microwave, uncovered, at High (100%) for 1 to 2 minutes or until peppers are softened.

2. Blend in flour, dry mustard and a pinch each of salt and pepper. Microwave, uncovered, at High (100%) for 30 seconds. Gradually stir in Milk until smooth. Microwave, uncovered, at High (100%) for 3 to 5 minutes or until mixture comes to a boil and thickens. Stir at least once during cooking.

3. Stir in ham, cover and microwave at High (100%) for 2 to 3 minutes or until heated through. Stir in sour cream. Season to taste with salt and pepper.

4. Spoon over toasted English muffins.

Serves 4.

CHICKEN BREASTS IN CREAMY DIJON MUSTARD SAUCE

A quick and simple recipe for those days when dinner has to be on the table in a hurry. Serve with rice or noodles and microwaved broccoli or green beans.

1 tbsp.	butter	15	mL
1	onion, chopped	1	
1 tsp.	chicken stock mix	5	mL
1/3 cup	water	75	mL
6	single chicken breasts, skinned and boned, flattened slightly	6	
1 cup	Milk	250	mL
1 tbsp.	flour	15	mL
1/4 cup	Dijon mustard	50	mL
	salt and pepper		
	sliced toasted almonds		

1. Combine butter and onion in a shallow microwavable dish that holds the chicken breasts in a single layer. Microwave, uncovered, at High (100%) for 2 to 4 minutes or until onion is softened. Stir partway through.

2. Stir chicken stock mix and water into dish; arrange chicken breasts evenly over liquid, with thicker portions towards outer edges of dish. Cover with waxed paper and microwave at Medium-High (70%) for 12 to 14 minutes or until chicken is tender and no longer pink. Since chicken breasts vary greatly in size, microwave for the minimum time, then test–they should be tender and no longer pink when cut in centre, or juices should run clear when meat is pierced. Turn over partway through cooking. Transfer to a heated platter, cover to keep warm.

3. Combine Milk and flour until smooth. Whisk into liquid in dish. Micro-wave, uncovered, at High (100%) for 4 to 6 minutes or until mixture boils and thickens. Whisk twice during cooking. Blend in mustard and season to taste with salt and pepper.

4. To serve, pour sauce over chicken and garnish with almonds.

Serves 6.

CITRUS GLAZED CHICKEN

A delightful chicken dish for just the two of you. Serve with cooked rice or noodles and microwaved broccoli.

1 tbsp.	butter	15 mL
1	green onion, chopped	1
1	clove garlic, minced	1
1/2 tsp.	chopped fresh ginger root (or a pinch of ground ginger)	2 mL
2	single chicken breasts, skinned and boned	2
1/2 tsp.	grated lemon peel	2 mL
1/2 tsp.	grated orange peel	2 mL
1 tbsp.	lemon juice	15 mL
1 tbsp.	orange juice	15 mL
1 tbsp.	flour	15 mL
3/4 cup	Milk	175 mL
1 tsp.	Chinese "hoisin" sauce, optional	5 mL
1 tbsp.	chopped fresh parsley	15 mL
	salt and pepper	
1/2	lemon or orange, sliced	1/2

1. Melt butter in a shallow microwavable dish that will hold the chicken breasts in a single layer, such as a glass pie plate, at High (100%) for 30 to 40 seconds. Stir in onion, garlic and ginger, and microwave, uncovered, at High (100%) for 30 seconds or until vegetables are softened.

2. Coat both sides of chicken with butter mixture, then arrange thicker portions towards outer edges of dish. Sprinkle lemon and orange peels and juices over chicken. Cover with waxed paper and microwave at Medium-High (70%) for 3 to 5 minutes or until chicken is tender and no longer pink. Turn over partway through cooking. Transfer to a plate, cover to keep warm.

3. Whisk flour into liquid in dish until smooth. Microwave, uncovered, at High (100%) for 20 seconds. Gradually whisk in Milk until smooth. Microwave, uncovered, at High (100%) for 2 to 4 minutes or until mixture comes to a boil and thickens slightly. Whisk once or twice during cooking. Stir in hoisin, if using, parsley and salt and pepper to taste.

4. Spoon sauce over chicken and garnish with lemon or orange slices. Serves 2.

SWISS CHICKEN DIVAN

A quick meal for leftover chicken or turkey. Frozen broccoli could be used in place of fresh, just microwave according to package directions.

1	stalk broccoli	1
2 tbsp.	butter	30 mL
3 tbsp.	flour	45 mL
2 tsp.	chicken stock mix	10 mL
1/2 tsp.	dry mustard	2 mL
1 1/2 cups	Milk	375 mL
	salt and pepper	
3/4 cup	shredded Swiss cheese	175 mL
2 cups	cubed cooked chicken	500 mL
	shredded Swiss cheese	
	paprika	

1. Trim broccoli into florets, leaving about 2 inches (5 cm) on each stem. Wash well and arrange in a 11 x 7 inch (2 L) microwavable dish with stems towards outer edges of dish. Cover with vented plastic wrap and microwave at High (100%) for 4 to 6 minutes or until tender. Let stand, covered.

2. Melt butter in a 4 cup (1 L) glass measure at High (100%) for 30 to 50 seconds. Blend in flour, chicken stock mix and dry mustard. Microwave at High (100%) for 30 seconds. Gradually whisk in Milk until smooth. Microwave, uncovered, at High (100%) for 4 to 6 minutes or until mixture comes to a boil and thickens. Whisk twice during cooking. Season to taste with salt and pepper. Stir in 3/4 cup (175 mL) cheese until melted, then add chicken.

3. Drain off any liquid from broccoli. Pour sauce over broccoli and sprinkle with additional Swiss cheese. Dust lightly with paprika. Run under preheated broiler until cheese is melted and bubbly, if desired.

Serves 3 to 4.

COCONUT CURRIED CHICKEN

This creamy coconut curry sauce is wonderful spooned over the chicken and served with rice or noodles.

1 cup	Milk	250 mL
1/2 cup	shredded coconut	125 mL
6	chicken thighs, about 1-1/2 lbs. (750 g)	6
2 tbsp.	butter	30 mL
1	onion, chopped	1
1	clove garlic, minced	1
1 tsp.	chopped fresh ginger root	5 mL
1 tbsp.	curry powder	15 mL
1 tsp.	ground coriander	5 mL
2 tbsp.	lemon juice	30 mL
1 tbsp.	cornstarch	15 mL
	salt and pepper	

1. Microwave Milk at High (100%) for 2 minutes or until hot but not boiling. Pour over coconut in a small bowl and let stand.

2. Trim excess fat off chicken pieces and pierce skin in several places with a fork. Set aside.

3. Combine butter, onion, garlic and ginger in a shallow microwavable dish that holds the chicken pieces in a single layer. Microwave, uncovered, at High (100%) for 2 to 3 minutes or until onion is softened. Stir partway through cooking.

4. Stir curry powder, coriander and lemon juice into onion mixture until smooth. Coat both sides of chicken pieces in curry mixture, then arrange evenly in dish, with thicker portions towards outer edges of dish. Cover with waxed paper and microwave at Medium-High (70%) for 10 to 14 minutes or until chicken is tender and juices run clear when meat is pierced. Turn over partway through cooking. Transfer chicken to a plate and cover to keep warm.

5. Stir about 1/4 cup (50 mL) of the coconut Milk mixture into cornstarch in a small bowl, until evenly blended. Stir into juices in dish, along with the rest of the coconut Milk. Microwave, uncovered, at High (100%) for 3 to 5 minutes or until mixture comes to a boil and thickens. Stir often during cooking.

6. Serve sauce over chicken pieces.

Serves 4.

POACHED CHICKEN WITH MUSHROOMS

Serve with small boiled potatoes and julienne carrots.

1 1/2 cups	sliced fresh mushrooms	375 mL
4	green onions, sliced	4
4	single chicken breasts, skinned	4
	paprika and pepper	
1/4 cup	dry white wine, vermouth,	50 mL
	or chicken stock	
1 tbsp.	flour	15 mL
1/2 cup	Milk	125 mL
1/4 tsp.	dried tarragon	1 mL
1 tbsp.	chopped fresh parsley	15 mL
	salt and pepper	

1. Sprinkle mushrooms and green onions evenly in a shallow micro-wavable dish that holds the chicken pieces in a single layer. Rub chicken breasts lightly with paprika and pepper and arrange bone side down with thicker portions towards outer edges of dish. Pour wine over all and cover with waxed paper. Microwave at Medium-High (70%) for 10 to 14 minutes, turning over partway through cooking until chicken is tender and no longer pink when meat is cut.

2. Carefully pour poaching liquid into a 2 cup (500 mL) glass measure. Blend in flour. Gradually whisk in Milk until smooth. Microwave, uncovered, at High (100%) for 2 to 4 minutes or until mixture comes to a boil and thickens. Whisk at least once during cooking. Stir in tarragon, parsley and salt and pepper to taste.

3. To serve, pour sauce over chicken pieces and top with mushrooms and green onions.

Serves 4.

BREADED CHICKEN AND HERBED CHEESE

Chicken is always moist in the microwave and this breading seals in the flavourful juices. The herb cheese makes a creamy and very garlicky dish!

1/4 cup	fine dry breadcrumbs	50	mL
1/4 cup	ground almonds	50	mL
1	113.4 g package Rondele cheese (cream cheese with garlic and herbs)	1	
1 tbsp.	Milk	15	mL
4	single chicken breasts, skinned and boned	4	
1 tbsp.	butter	15	mL
2	green onions, chopped	2	
1	clove garlic, minced	1	
1 tbsp.	flour	15	mL
3/4 cup	Milk	175	mL
	pepper		

1. Combine breadcrumbs and ground almonds in a glass pie plate. Microwave, uncovered, at High (100%) for 3 to 5 minutes or until lightly golden. Stir every minute. Watch carefully to avoid scorching. Set aside.

2. In another pie plate or shallow dish, beat cheese and Milk together until smooth.

3. Press chicken breasts first in cheese mixture, coating both sides, then in breadcrumb mixture, coating both sides. Arrange evenly on a micro-wave roasting rack with thicker portions towards outer edges. Microwave, uncovered, at Medium (50%) for 8 to 10 minutes or until chicken is firm to the touch. Rotate rack, as necessary, for even cooking. Let stand while making sauce.

4. Combine butter, green onions and garlic in a 4 cup (1 L) glass measure and microwave, uncovered, at High (100%) for 1 minute or until softened. Blend in flour and microwave, uncovered at High (100%) for 20 seconds. Gradually whisk in Milk until smooth. Microwave, uncovered, at High (100%) for 2 to 4 minutes or until mixture comes to a boil and thickens. Whisk at least once during cooking. Whisk in remaining cheese until smooth. Season to taste with pepper. Thin sauce, if necessary, with a little Milk.

5. Serve chicken with sauce spooned over the top.

Serves 4.

TURKEY FAJITA CASSEROLE

The cheese sauce is just a little nippy from the hot red pepper flakes. If you like peppery "heat", substitute 1 tbsp. (15 mL) chopped hot banana or jalapeno pepper.

4	slices bacon	4
2 tbsp.	butter	30 mL
4	green onions, sliced	4
1/2	red pepper, thinly sliced	1/2
1 cup	thinly sliced cooked turkey	250 mL
2	cloves garlic, minced	2
1/2 tsp.	grated lime peel	2 mL
1	7 1/2 oz. (213 mL) can pizza sauce	1
4	6 inch (15 cm) flour tortillas	4
Sauce		
2 tbsp.	butter	30 mL
2 tbsp.	chopped red or green pepper	30 mL
1/2 tsp.	dried basil	2 mL
pinch	hot red pepper flakes	pinch
2 tbsp.	flour	30 mL
1 cup	Milk	250 mL
1 cup	shredded Cheddar cheese	250 mL
	salt and pepper	

1. Trim as much fat from bacon as possible and cut into 2 inch (5 cm) pieces. Spread evenly between double thickness of paper towel. Microwave at High (100%) for 2 to 3 minutes or until crisp. Set aside.

2. Combine butter, onions, red pepper, turkey, garlic and lime peel in a shallow 8 inch (20 cm) square microwavable baking dish. Microwave, uncovered, at High (100%) for 3 to 4 minutes or until vegetables are softened. Transfer to a bowl and set aside.

3. Spread each tortilla with 1 tbsp. (15 mL) of pizza sauce. Dividing evenly, spoon turkey mixture onto each tortilla. Divide bacon evenly over tortillas and roll up.

4. Spread remaining pizza sauce in bottom of baking dish and place tortillas, seam side down on sauce. Cover with plastic wrap to prevent drying out while making cheese sauce.

5. Combine butter, red or green pepper, basil and hot red pepper flakes in a 2 cup (500 mL) glass measure and microwave, uncovered, at High (100%) for 1 to 2 minutes or until pepper is softened. Blend in flour and microwave at High (100%) for 30 seconds.

Continued on next page

TURKEY FAJITA CASSEROLE

(Continued)

6. Gradually whisk in Milk until smooth. Microwave, uncovered, at High (100%) for 3 to 5 minutes or until mixture comes to a boil and thickens. Whisk at least once during cooking. Stir in cheese until melted. Season to taste with salt and pepper.

7. Pour half the sauce over the tortillas. Cover with vented plastic wrap and microwave at High (100%) for 3 to 4 minutes or until heated through. Let stand, covered for 2 minutes.

8. Serve remaining sauce separately.

Serves 4.

TURKEY TETRAZZINI

A perfect way to use leftovers, this attractive dish is great when you want a satisfying supper that's light on meat.

2 cups	penne pasta	500 mL
1/4 cup	butter, divided	50 mL
1 cup	sliced fresh mushrooms	250 mL
1/2 cup	thinly sliced green onions	125 mL
1	stalk celery, chopped	1
2 tbsp.	flour	30 mL
1 cup	Milk	250 mL
1/2 cup	undiluted canned chicken stock	125 mL
	nutmeg	
1 cup	cubed cooked turkey	250 mL
	salt and pepper	
2	large tomatoes	2
2 tbsp.	grated Parmesan cheese	30 mL

1. Cook penne conventionally according to package directions until al dente (tender but firm).

2. Combine 3 tbsp. (45 mL) butter, mushrooms, green onions and celery in an 8 cup (2 L) microwavable casserole. Microwave, uncovered, at High (100%) for 3 to 4 minutes or until vegetables are softened. Blend in flour and microwave, uncovered, at High (100%) for 30 seconds.

3. Gradually whisk in Milk, chicken stock and a pinch of nutmeg until smooth. Microwave, uncovered, at High (100%) for 4 to 6 minutes or until mixture comes to a boil and thickens. Whisk once or twice during cooking.

4. Stir in penne and turkey. Season to taste with salt and pepper. Peel tomato; cut into thick slices and remove seeds. Arrange slices over casserole.

5. Melt remaining 1 tbsp. (15 mL) butter at High (100%) for 20 to 30 seconds. Brush over tomatoes, then sprinkle with cheese. Cover and microwave at High (100%) for 3 to 5 minutes or until heated through.

Serves 4.

TURKEY POT PIE

So easy to make and so tasty, this pie could become a post-Christmas tradition. To keep the onions intact as they cook, cut a small cross in the root ends.

2 tbsp.	butter	30	mL
6	onions, about 1 inch (2.5 cm) in diameter	6	
2	slender carrots, thickly sliced	2	
1	medium potato, cut in 1 inch (2.5 cm) pieces	1	
2 tbsp.	flour	30	mL
1 cup	undiluted canned chicken stock	250	mL
2/3 cup	Milk	150	mL
2 tbsp.	chopped fresh parsley	30	mL
1/2 tsp.	dried savory	2	mL
	pepper		
2 cups	cubed cooked turkey	500	mL
1/2 cup	frozen peas	125	mL
Crust			
2 cups	tea biscuit mix	500	mL
1/2 cup	shredded Cheddar cheese	125	mL
1/2 cup	Milk (approx.)	125	mL

1. Combine butter, onions, carrots and potatoes in an 8 cup (2 L) microwavable casserole. Cover and microwave at High (100%) for 4 to 6 minutes or until vegetables are tender crisp. Blend in flour and microwave at High (100%) for 1 minute.

2. Gradually whisk in chicken stock and Milk until smooth. Cover and microwave at High (100%) for 4 to 6 minutes or until mixture comes to a boil and thickens slightly. Whisk twice during cooking. Stir in parsley, savory and pepper to taste. Add turkey and peas. Set aside.

3. Combine biscuit mix and half the cheese. With a fork, stir in just enough Milk to make a soft, sticky dough. Turn out onto a floured board and knead 5 or 6 times. Pat into a circle to fit casserole.

4. Place dough into casserole and score deeply into pie-shaped wedges with a sharp knife. Press dough back from centre to leave a 2 inch (5 cm) vent in centre. Sprinkle remaining cheese on top. Microwave, uncovered, at High (100%) for 4 to 6 minutes or until top is puffed and firm to the touch and the filling is hot.

5. Let stand for 5 minutes before serving.

Serves 4 to 6.

MOUSSAKA

Substitute lean ground beef for lamb if you prefer. Serve with crusty rolls and a marinated vegetable salad.

1	medium eggplant, about 1 lb. (500 g)	1	
1 tbsp.	salt	15	mL
Meat Sauce			
1 lb.	ground lamb	500	g
1	onion, chopped	1	
1	5 1/2 oz. (156 mL) can tomato paste	1	
1/2 cup	dry red wine or beef stock	125	mL
1 tsp.	cinnamon	5	mL
1/2 tsp.	dried oregano	2	mL
1/4 tsp.	salt	1	mL
1/4 tsp.	pepper	1	mL
White Sauce			
2 tbsp.	butter	30	mL
2 tbsp.	flour	30	mL
1/4 tsp.	nutmeg	1	mL
pinch	salt and pepper	pinch	
1 cup	Milk	250	mL
1	egg, lightly beaten	1	
2 tbsp.	grated Parmesan cheese	30	mL
1 tbsp.	dry breadcrumbs	15	mL

1. Cut eggplant crosswise into 1/2 inch (1 cm) slices. Place in colander and sprinkle with salt. Let stand to drain for 20 minutes.

2. Crumble lamb and onion in an 8 cup (2 L) microwavable casserole. Microwave, uncovered, at High (100%) for 4 to 6 minutes or until lamb is no longer pink. Stir twice to break up lumps. Drain off fat.

3. Stir in tomato paste, wine, cinnamon, oregano, salt and pepper. Cover and microwave at High (100%) for 2 to 3 minutes or until mixture comes to a boil. Stir and continue microwaving at Medium (50%) for 5 to 7 minutes or until slightly thickened. Stir once during cooking. Set aside.

4. Melt butter in a 4 cup (1 L) glass measure at High (100%) for 30 to 50 seconds. Blend in flour, nutmeg, salt and pepper and microwave at High (100%) for 30 seconds. Gradually stir in Milk until smooth. Microwave, uncovered, at High (100%) for 3 to 5 minutes or until mixture comes to a boil and thickens. Stir at least once during cooking.

Continued on next page

MOUSSAKA

(Continued)

Stir a little of the hot sauce into beaten egg, blending well. Return warmed egg to sauce and microwave, uncovered, at Medium (50%) for 30 to 60 seconds or until thickened. Stir in Parmesan cheese until melted. Set aside.

5. Rinse eggplant under cold running water. Drain on paper towel and pat dry. Arrange evenly in a round 8 cup (2 L) microwavable casserole. Cover and microwave at High (100%) for 3 to 5 minutes or until tender. Drain well. Remove eggplant.

6. Sprinkle breadcrumbs in same round 8 cup (2 L) microwavable casserole. Arrange half the eggplant slices over bottom; top with meat mixture. Cover with remaining eggplant, then white sauce.

7. Cover and microwave at Medium-High (70%) for 12 to 16 minutes or until heated through. Rotate dish, if necessary, but do not stir. Let stand, covered, for 5 to 10 minutes before serving.

Serves 4.

LAMB CASHEW CURRY

The lamb cubes are quickly sautéed on the stove top for colour and to seal in the juices. Serve over rice or noodles and with a green vegetable.

1 lb.	boneless, lean lamb, cut into 3/4 inch (2 cm) cubes	500 g
2 tbsp.	vegetable oil	30 mL
2 tbsp.	butter	30 mL
1	onion, chopped	1
2	stalks celery, chopped	2
2	cloves garlic, minced	2
2 tbsp.	flour	30 mL
2 tsp.	chicken stock mix	10 mL
1 1/2 tsp.	curry powder	7 mL
1 tsp.	ground cumin	5 mL
1/8 tsp.	cayenne	0.5 mL
1 1/2 cups	Milk	375 mL
1/2 cup	chopped cashews	125 mL
1	medium ripe tomato, chopped	1
	salt and pepper	

1. Heat oil in a large skillet on stove top. Brown lamb cubes evenly on all sides. Set aside.

2. Combine butter, onion, celery and garlic in an 8 cup (2 L) microwavable casserole. Microwave, uncovered, at High (100%) for 3 to 4 minutes or until vegetables are tender. Blend in flour, chicken stock mix, curry, cumin and cayenne and microwave, uncovered, at High (100%) for 30 seconds. Gradually stir in Milk until smooth. Microwave, uncovered, at High (100%) for 4 to 6 minutes or until mixture comes to a boil and thickens. Stir at least once during cooking.

3. Stir in lamb, cover and microwave at High (100%) for 4 minutes. Stir and microwave at Medium (50%) for 12 to 16 minutes or until lamb is tender. Stir twice during cooking.

4. Add cashews and tomato and let stand, covered, for 5 minutes. Season to taste with salt and pepper.

Serves 4.

SOLE TURBANS WITH LEMON DILL SAUCE

These individual rice-stuffed fish turbans are impressive enough for guests and easy enough for everyday meals.

1/3 cup	long grain rice	75 mL
2/3 cup	chicken stock or water	150 mL
1	lemon	1
2 tsp.	chopped fresh parsley	10 mL
1/2 tsp.	salt	2 mL
pinch	dried thyme and pepper	pinch
4	sole fillets, about 1 lb. (500 g)	4
	salt and pepper	

Sauce

2 tbsp.	butter	30 mL
2 tbsp.	flour	30 mL
1/4 tsp.	salt	1 mL
1 1/4 cups	Milk	300 mL
1 1/2 tsp.	chopped fresh dill	7 mL
1/2 tsp.	lemon juice	2 mL
	lemon slices and dill	

1. Combine rice and chicken stock or water in a 6 cup (1.5 L) microwavable casserole. Cover and microwave at High (100%) for 8 to 10 minutes or until most of the liquid is absorbed. Stir and let stand, covered, for 3 minutes.

2. Grate peel from lemon and set aside. Peel lemon, remove any pith and dice flesh. Stir diced lemon, lemon peel, parsley, salt, thyme and pepper into rice. Set aside.

3. Wipe fillets well and sprinkle with salt and pepper. Line sides and bottom of four 6 oz. (175 mL) custard cups with fish. Fill each cup with rice.

4. Cover with waxed paper and arrange in a circle in microwave oven, about 2 inches (5 cm) apart. Microwave at High (100%) for 4 to 6 minutes or until fish is opaque and flakes easily with a fork. Let stand, covered, while making sauce.

Continued on next page

SOLE TURBANS WITH LEMON DILL SAUCE

(Continued)

5. Melt butter in a 4 cup (1 L) glass measure at High (100%) for 30 to 50 seconds. Blend in flour and salt and microwave at High (100%) for 30 seconds. Gradually whisk in Milk until smooth. Microwave, uncovered, at High (100%) for 3 to 5 minutes or until mixture comes to a boil and thickens. Whisk once or twice during cooking. Stir in lemon and dill.

6. Drain off any liquid on fish. To serve, invert turbans on serving plates, pour sauce over and garnish with lemon slices and dill.

Serves 4.

BAKED FISH CREOLE

Delicious enough to make fish lovers of everyone! For the most delicate flavour, use fresh, white-fleshed fish fillets.

2 tbsp.	butter	30 mL
1	onion, chopped	1
1	clove garlic, minced	1
2	stalks celery, chopped	2
1	green pepper, chopped	1
1/4 cup	flour	50 mL
2 cups	Milk	500 mL
1 tsp.	salt	5 mL
1/4 tsp.	pepper	1 mL
1/2 tsp.	Tabasco sauce (or more to taste)	2 mL
1/2 cup	chili sauce	125 mL
3 cups	cooked rice	750 mL
1 lb.	thin fish fillets	500 g
2	tomatoes, sliced	2

1. Combine butter, onion, garlic, celery and green pepper in an 8 cup (2 L) glass measure or microwavable casserole. Microwave, uncovered, at High (100%) for 4 to 6 minutes or until tender.

2. Blend in flour and microwave, uncovered, at High (100%) for 1 minute. Gradually whisk in Milk until smooth. Cover and microwave at High (100%) for 5 to 7 minutes or until mixture comes to a boil and thickens. Whisk twice during cooking. Season with salt, pepper, Tabasco and chili sauce and microwave at High (100%) for 1 to 3 minutes or until hot.

3. Place cooked rice in bottom of a 12 x 8 inch (3 L) glass baking dish. Arrange fish on top with the thicker portions towards the outer edges of the dish. Arrange tomatoes on top of fish and cover with sauce. Cover with waxed paper and microwave at High (100%) for 5 to 8 minutes or until fish is opaque and flakes easily with a fork. Rotate dish, as necessary, during cooking. Let stand a few minutes before serving.

Serves 4.

SEAFOOD KEBOBS
WITH LEMON SAUCE

Choose a firm fish such as swordfish, salmon, cod or halibut. You can vary the seafood, but keep the amounts about the same. This can also be served as an appetizer for eight.

1/2 lb.	firm fish steak, about 1 inch (2.5 cm) thick	250 g
8	large (but not tiger) shrimp, peeled and deveined	8
8	sea scallops	8
1	green pepper, cut into 1 inch (2.5 cm) squares	1
1/2	Spanish onion, cut into pieces	1/2
8	cherry tomatoes	8
Marinade		
1/2 cup	vegetable oil	125 mL
1/4 cup	lemon juice	50 mL
1	green onion, chopped	1
1/2 tsp.	dried tarragon	2 mL
Lemon Sauce		
2 tbsp.	butter	30 mL
1 tbsp.	flour	15 mL
1 cup	Milk	250 mL
2 tsp.	Dijon mustard	10 mL
1/2 tsp.	salt	2 mL
	pepper	
1/2 tsp.	grated lemon peel	2 mL
2 tbsp.	lemon juice	30 mL
1 tbsp.	chopped fresh parsley	15 mL

1. Cut fish into 1 inch (2.5 cm) pieces. Thread fish, shrimp, scallops, green pepper, onion and cherry tomatoes alternately on bamboo skewers, leaving a small space between each piece for even cooking. Combine marinade ingredients and pour over kebobs. Cover and marinate in refrigerator for 2 hours.

2. Make sauce by melting butter in a 4 cup (1 L) glass measure at High (100%) for 30 to 50 seconds. Blend in flour and microwave at High (100%) for 20 seconds. Gradually whisk in Milk until smooth. Microwave, uncovered, at High (100%) for 3 to 5 minutes or until mixture comes to a boil and thickens. Whisk twice during cooking. Add mustard, salt, pepper to taste, lemon peel, lemon juice and parsley. Cover and set Lemon Sauce aside.

Continued on next page

SEAFOOD KEBOBS WITH LEMON SAUCE
(Continued)

3. Remove kebobs from marinade and place in a shallow dish, spacing out evenly. Cover with waxed paper and microwave at High (100%) for 6 to 8 minutes or until shrimp turns pink and scallops are opaque. Rearrange skewers partway through cooking. It may be necessary to do this in two batches for even cooking and as space permits. If so, divide cooking time accordingly.

4. Serve with Lemon Sauce, reheating if necessary.

Serves 4.

PRONTO SHRIMP CURRY

This is a mild curry, so for more spice increase curry as desired. Serve over rice with your choice of condiments. Leftover cooked meat such as chicken or lamb may be substituted.

2 tbsp.	butter	30 mL
1	small onion, chopped	1
1	small stalk celery, chopped	1
1	clove garlic, minced	1
3 tbsp.	flour	45 mL
1 tsp.	curry powder	5 mL
1 tsp.	chicken stock mix or chicken bouillon cube, crushed	5 mL
2 cups	Milk	500 mL
2 cups	cooked shrimp	500 mL
	salt and pepper	
	hot cooked rice	
	assorted condiments–chutney, coconut, yogurt, peanuts or raisins	

1. Combine butter, onion, celery and garlic in a 6 cup (1.5 L) micro-wavable casserole. Microwave, uncovered, at High (100%) for 2 to 4 minutes or until vegetables are tender. Blend in flour, curry and chicken stock mix or cube. Microwave, uncovered, at High (100%) for 30 seconds.

2. Gradually whisk in Milk until smooth. Cover and microwave at High (100%) for 5 to 7 minutes or until mixture comes to a boil and thickens. Whisk twice during cooking.

3. Stir in shrimp and microwave at High (100%) for 1 to 2 minutes or until heated through. Season to taste with salt and pepper.

4. Serve over rice along with condiments.

Serves 4.

SALMON LOAF WITH DILL AND PARSLEY SAUCE

A lightly flavoured cream herb sauce is a pleasing contrast to the slightly spicy salmon loaf. For an attractive presentation, turn loaf out onto serving plate and garnish with dill and lemon slices.

2	7 1/2 oz. (213 g) cans pink salmon	2
2 tbsp.	butter	30 mL
1/4 cup	finely chopped celery	50 mL
2 tbsp.	finely chopped onion	30 mL
1 tbsp.	flour	15 mL
1/2 cup	Milk	125 mL
1/2 cup	dry breadcrumbs	125 mL
1/4 cup	tomato sauce	50 mL
2 tsp.	Worcestershire sauce	10 mL
dash	Tabasco sauce	dash
	salt and pepper	

Sauce

4 tsp.	butter	20 mL
4 tsp.	flour	20 mL
1 cup	Milk	250 mL
1/2 tsp.	grated lemon peel	2 mL
2 tbsp.	chopped fresh parsley	30 mL
2 tbsp.	chopped fresh dill	30 mL
	salt and pepper	

1. Drain salmon; reserve 1 tbsp. (15 mL) liquid. Remove and discard skin. Mash salmon and bones well, adding the 1 tbsp. (15 mL) salmon liquid. Set aside.

2. Combine butter, celery and onion in a 6 cup (1.5 L) microwavable soufflé dish or round casserole. Microwave, uncovered, at High (100%) for 1 to 2 minutes or until softened. Blend in flour and microwave, uncovered, at High (100%) for 20 seconds. Gradually whisk in Milk until smooth. Microwave, uncovered, at High (100%) for 2 to 4 minutes or until mixture comes to a boil and thickens. Whisk at least once during cooking.

3. Stir in breadcrumbs, tomato sauce, Worcestershire sauce and Tabasco. Add salmon, blending well and season to taste with salt and pepper. Smooth top until even with a fork. Cover with waxed paper and microwave at Medium-High (70%) for 6 minutes. Uncover and microwave at High (100%) for 2 to 5 minutes or until edges and top are firm and centre is almost set. Let stand, covered, while making sauce.

Continued on next page

SALMON LOAF WITH DILL AND PARSLEY SAUCE

(Continued)

4. Melt butter in a 2 cup (500 mL) glass measure at High (100%) for 30 to 40 seconds. Blend in flour and microwave, uncovered, at High (100%) for 20 seconds. Gradually whisk in Milk until smooth. Microwave, uncovered, at High (100%) for 3 to 5 minutes or until mixture comes to a boil and thickens. Whisk once or twice.

5. Stir in lemon peel, parsley and dill. Microwave, uncovered, at High (100%) for 30 seconds. Season to taste with salt and pepper.

6. To serve, run knife around edge of salmon loaf. Turn loaf out onto serving plate and garnish with dill and lemon slices, if desired. Cut into wedges and serve with sauce.

Serves 4 to 6.

TUNA POTATO CASSEROLE

This casserole has a pleasing contrast of tender and crunchy vegetables.

2 tbsp.	butter	30 mL
2	green onions, chopped	2
1	large stalk celery, sliced	1
1/2	red pepper, chopped	1/2
1/2 cup	Milk	125 mL
2 cups	large diced potatoes	500 mL
1/2 tsp.	dried oregano	2 mL
1/2 tsp.	salt	2 mL
pinch	nutmeg	pinch
1/2 cup	shredded Cheddar cheese	125 mL
1	7 1/2 oz. (213 g) water or broth packed tuna	1
1/2 cup	frozen peas, thawed	125 mL
	salt and pepper	

1. Melt butter in an 8 cup (2 L) microwavable casserole at High (100%) for 1 minute or until sizzling. Stir in onions, celery and red pepper. Microwave, uncovered, at High (100%) for 2 to 3 minutes or until softened. Transfer with a slotted spoon to a plate and set aside.

2. To remaining butter in casserole add Milk, potatoes, oregano, salt and nutmeg. Cover and microwave at High (100%) for 6 to 8 minutes or until potatoes are tender. Let stand, covered, for 5 minutes.

3. Stir in cheese until melted. Break tuna into large flakes and add to potatoes along with reserved vegetables and peas. Season to taste with salt and pepper.

4. Microwave, uncovered, at High (100%) for 2 to 3 minutes or until heated through.

Serves 4.

POLENTA TUNA PIZZA

Polenta, a popular corn meal staple of Northern Italy, makes a tender crust for this pizza.

1/2 cup	cornmeal	125 mL
1/2 tsp.	salt	2 mL
1/2 tsp.	baking powder	2 mL
pinch	hot red pepper flakes, optional	pinch
1 cup	Milk	250 mL
1/2 cup	water	125 mL
2 tbsp.	butter	30 mL
1	large tomato, peeled, seeded and chopped	1
2 tbsp.	chopped onion	30 mL
1/4 tsp.	dried oregano	1 mL
1	3.75 oz. (106 g) can water or broth packed tuna	1
1/4 cup	sliced black olives	50 mL
3/4 cup	shredded Monteray Jack or other mild cheese	175 mL

1. Combine cornmeal, salt, baking powder and hot red pepper flakes in a 9 1/2 inch (24 cm) deep dish glass pie plate or baking dish. Stir in Milk and water. Microwave, uncovered, at High (100%) for 8 to 10 minutes or until thick and set, stirring every 2 minutes. Set aside.

2. Combine butter, tomato, onion and oregano in a small microwavable bowl. Microwave, uncovered, at High (100%) for 2 to 3 minutes or until onion is softened.

3. Drain tuna well and break up into flakes. Add to tomato mixture with olives and mix gently. Spoon mixture evenly over cornmeal base. Sprinkle with cheese and microwave, uncovered, at High (100%) for 2 to 3 minutes or until cheese melts.

Serves 4 to 6.

TURBOT WITH SPINACH PESTO CASSEROLE

The spinach and basil pesto provides a wonderful contrast to the delicate flavour of turbot or sole fillets.

8 cups	torn, washed spinach	2	L
3 tbsp.	butter, divided	45	mL
1/2 cup	thinly sliced green onions	125	mL
3/4 cup	fresh breadcrumbs	175	mL
1/4 cup	torn, fresh basil leaves	50	mL
1/4 cup	grated Parmesan cheese	50	mL
1/2 cup	Milk	125	mL
	salt and pepper		
1 lb.	turbot or sole fillets, thawed if frozen	500	g
1/2 cup	toasted, buttered breadcrumbs*	125	mL

1. Place spinach in an 8 cup (2 L) microwavable casserole or bowl. Cover and microwave at High (100%) for 3 to 4 minutes or until tender. Let stand, covered, until cool, then drain in colander and squeeze as dry as possible. Chop finely and set aside.

2. Combine 2 tbsp. (30 mL) of the butter and green onions in a shallow microwavable dish that holds fish in a single layer. Microwave, uncovered, at High (100%) for 1 to 2 minutes or until onion is softened. Stir in breadcrumbs, coating well, then basil, cheese and Milk. Mix to a paste-like consistency. Stir in spinach and spread evenly in bottom of dish.

3. Pat fillets thoroughly dry with paper towels and arrange over spinach mixture in a single layer with thickest parts of fillets towards outer edges of dish. Spread with remaining 1 tbsp. (15 mL) butter and season lightly with salt and pepper.

4. Cover with vented plastic wrap and microwave at High (100%) for 4 to 6 minutes or until fish is opaque and flakes easily with a fork. Carefully pour off any accumulated liquid from dish.

5. Sprinkle with buttered crumbs and microwave, uncovered, at High (100%) for 1 minute.

Serves 4.

* To toast breadcrumbs, melt 2 tsp. (10 mL) butter in a shallow microwavable dish such as a glass pie plate at High (100%) for 20 to 30 seconds. Stir in 1/2 cup (125 mL) fresh breadcrumbs, coating with butter. Microwave, uncovered, at High (100%) for 2 to 4 minutes or until lightly golden and quite dry. Stir often to break up and prevent scorching. Let stand until cool. (They will continue to crisp up during standing time).

KEDGEREE

A traditional hearty British breakfast dish, kedgeree makes a very tasty brunch or supper dish that's easy to make in the microwave.

1 cup	long grain rice	250 mL
1 1/2 cups	water	375 mL
1 lb.	smoked cod or finnan haddie	500 g
2 tbsp.	butter	30 mL
1	small onion, chopped	1
1	bay leaf	1
3/4 cup	Milk, divided	175 mL
pinch	mace	pinch
1/4 cup	light cream	50 mL
2 tbsp.	chopped fresh parsley	30 mL
	salt and pepper	

1. Combine rice and water in an 8 cup (2 L) microwavable casserole. Cover and microwave at High (100%) for 5 to 8 minutes. Rice should be slightly undercooked. It will absorb remaining water during standing time. Let stand, covered.

2. Remove any skin from fish and cut into 2 inch (5 cm) pieces; set aside.

3. Combine butter and onion in a shallow 10 inch (25 cm) round microwavable dish and microwave, uncovered, at High (100%) for 1 to 2 minutes or until softened. Stir in bay leaf, 1/2 cup (125 mL) of the Milk and mace. Arrange fish with thickest pieces towards outer edge of dish. Cover with vented plastic wrap and microwave at Medium-High (70%) for 4 to 6 minutes or until fish flakes easily with a fork. Rotate dish, as necessary during cooking. Remove fish with slotted spoon and set aside.

4. Stir in remaining Milk and cream, then rice. Cover with vented plastic wrap and microwave at High (100%) for 3 to 5 minutes or until rice is tender. Stir partway through cooking.

5. Discard bay leaf. Stir in parsley and salt and pepper to taste. Gently add fish and microwave, covered, at High (100%) for 1 to 2 minutes or until heated through.

Serves 4 to 6.

SCALLOPS IN HERBED CREAM SAUCE WITH WHITE WINE

To add a touch of colour to this delicate seafood dish, serve with asparagus, lightly grilled cherry tomatoes and garnish with parsley.

1 lb.	medium sea scallops	500	g
3 tbsp.	butter, divided	45	mL
1	clove garlic, minced	1	
3	green onions, thinly sliced	3	
1/4 cup	dry white wine	50	mL
4 tsp.	flour	20	mL
3/4 cup	Milk	175	mL
3/4 cup	shredded Emmenthal cheese	175	mL
1 tbsp.	chopped fresh parsley	15	mL
1 tbsp.	chopped fresh dill	15	mL
	salt and white pepper		

1. Rinse scallops in cold water, pat dry with paper towel and set aside.

2. Combine half the butter, garlic and onions in a shallow 9 inch (23 cm) microwavable dish, such as a pie plate. Microwave, uncovered, at High (100%) for 2 to 3 minutes or until onions are softened.

3. Add scallops and wine, stirring gently into butter mixture. Cover with vented plastic wrap and microwave at Medium-High (70%) for 5 to 7 minutes or until scallops are just opaque. Stir gently partway through cooking. Uncover and set aside.

4. Melt remaining butter in a 2 cup (500 mL) glass measure at High (100%) for 30 to 40 seconds. Blend in flour and microwave, uncovered, at High (100%) for 20 seconds. Whisk in 1/4 cup (50 mL) of poaching liquid from scallops, then the Milk. Microwave, uncovered, at High (100%) for 3 to 5 minutes or until mixture comes to a boil and thickens. Whisk once during cooking. Stir in cheese until melted, then parsley, dill and salt and pepper to taste.

5. Pour any remaining liquid off scallops. Cover with sauce and microwave, uncovered, at Medium (50%) for 2 to 3 minutes or until heated through.

Serves 4.

PASTA, EGGS AND CHEESE

Tortellini with Tomato and
Parmesan Mushroom Sauce

Country Style Spaghetti

Pasta, Eggs and Cheese

These pasta recipes team a sauce made in the microwave with pasta cooked the traditional way on the stove. Take care to time the cooking of the pasta to coincide with the sauce. Prepare the sauce first, you can always reheat it, but not the pasta.

Cook pasta in a large pot that gives the pasta plenty of room to boil briskly, without being crowded. Cooking times for pasta vary according to the size and shape, but serving it 'al dente'—tender but firm—is recommended. The best way to find out if it's 'al dente' is to taste it often. When ready, drain the pasta in a colander, but don't rinse it. Transfer it to a warmed bowl and toss with the sauce.

Other light dishes in this section, suited to today's tastes and lifestyles, include Mushroom and Red Pepper Frittata, Chicken Leek and Mushroom Quiche, Bacon Cheese and Onion Tart, and Asparagus Rarebit. All of them make wonderful lunch, brunch or light supper dishes.

TORTELLINI WITH TOMATO AND PARMESAN MUSHROOM SAUCE

Cooked tortellini are tossed in a Parmesan mushroom sauce, then spooned over a tomato sauce. If you prefer, broil at the end for a golden finish.

3/4 lb.	fresh or frozen tortellini	375	g
3 tbsp.	butter, divided	45	mL
1	small onion, chopped	1	
2	cloves garlic, minced	2	
1	14 oz. (398 mL) can tomato sauce	1	
2 cups	sliced fresh mushrooms	500	mL
1/4 cup	chopped green onions	50	mL
2 tbsp.	flour	30	mL
2 cups	Milk	500	mL
2/3 cup	grated Parmesan cheese	150	mL
	salt and pepper		
1 1/2 cups	shredded mozzarella cheese	375	mL

1. Time the conventional cooking of the tortellini to coincide with the cooking of the sauce. Cook according to package directions until al dente (tender but firm). Drain.

2. Combine 1 tbsp. (15 mL) of the butter, onion and garlic in a 4 cup (1 L) glass measure or microwavable bowl. Microwave, uncovered, at High (100%) for 1 to 2 minutes or until tender. Add tomato sauce, cover and microwave at High (100%) for 3 to 4 minutes or until hot. Stir once. Cover and set aside.

3. Combine remaining 2 tbsp. (30 mL) butter, mushrooms and green onions in an 8 cup (2 L) glass measure or microwavable casserole. Microwave, uncovered, at High (100%) for 3 to 4 minutes or until mushrooms are tender.

4. Blend in flour and microwave, uncovered, at High (100%) for 30 seconds. Gradually stir in Milk until smooth. Microwave, uncovered, at High (100%) for 6 to 8 minutes or until mixture comes to a boil and thickens. Stir twice during cooking. Stir in Parmesan cheese until melted. Season to taste with salt and pepper.

5. Fold drained tortellini into mushroom Parmesan sauce.

6. Spread tomato sauce in 11 x 7 inch (2 L) microwavable baking dish. Top with tortellini mixture and sprinkle with mozzarella cheese. Microwave, uncovered, at High (100%) for 3 to 4 minutes or until cheese melts. Alternately, brown under conventional broiler until cheese is melted and golden.

Serves 4.

CHICKEN AND BROCCOLI CANNELLONI

This is a good make-ahead dish and ideal for toting. Assemble, cover and refrigerate. When ready to serve, add 2 to 4 minutes to the final cooking time at Medium-High (70%).

12	cannelloni or manicotti shells	12
Sauce		
1/3 cup	butter	75 mL
1/3 cup	flour	75 mL
3 cups	Milk	750 mL
1	28 oz. (796 mL) can plum tomatoes, drained and puréed or finely chopped salt and pepper	1
Filling		
3 tbsp.	butter	45 mL
1	large onion, chopped	1
2 cups	sliced fresh mushrooms	500 mL
1 1/2 cups	diced, cooked chicken (or turkey or ham)	375 mL
1 1/2 cups	chopped, cooked fresh broccoli	375 mL
1 cup	grated Parmesan cheese, divided salt and pepper	250 mL

1. Time the conventional cooking of the pasta to coincide with the finished sauce and filling. Cook according to package directions until al dente (tender but firm). Drain.

2. To make sauce, melt 1/3 cup (75 mL) butter in a 12 cup (3 L) microwavable casserole at High (100%) for 1 minute. Blend in flour and microwave, uncovered, at High (100%) for 1 minute. Gradually whisk in Milk until smooth. Cover and microwave at High (100%) for 8 to 10 minutes or until mixture comes to a boil and thickens. Whisk 2 or 3 times during cooking. Stir in tomatoes, cover and microwave at High (100%) for 2 to 4 minutes or until heated through. Season to taste with salt and pepper. Set aside.

3. For filling, combine 3 tbsp. (45 mL) butter, onion and mushrooms in another 12 cup (3 L) microwavable casserole or bowl. Microwave, uncovered, at High (100%) for 3 to 4 minutes or until vegetables are softened. Add chicken and broccoli. Add 1 cup (250 mL) sauce from above and 1/2 cup (125 mL) cheese. Blend well and fill cannelloni with mixture.

Continued on next page

CHICKEN AND BROCCOLI CANNELLONI

(Continued)

4. Arrange stuffed cannelloni in a 12 x 8 inch (3 L) microwavable casserole. Top with remaining sauce and cheese. Cover with vented plastic wrap and microwave at Medium-High (70%) for 12 to 16 minutes or until heated through. Rotate dish twice during cooking. Let stand, covered, for 5 to 10 minutes before serving.

Serves 6.

MANICOTTI WITH MUSHROOM SAUCE

Cheese-stuffed manicotti are smothered in a mushroom sauce and baked. Wonderful!

8	manicotti shells	8
Filling		
1 cup	ricotta cheese	250 mL
1 1/2 cups	shredded mozzarella cheese	375 mL
1/2 cup	grated Parmesan cheese	125 mL
2	eggs, lightly beaten	2
1/2 tsp.	dried basil	2 mL
1/2 tsp.	dried oregano	2 mL
	salt and pepper	
Sauce		
2 tbsp.	butter	30 mL
1	onion, chopped	1
1 cup	sliced fresh mushrooms	250 mL
3 tbsp.	flour	45 mL
1 tsp.	chicken stock mix	5 mL
1/4 tsp.	salt	1 mL
1/4 tsp.	pepper	1 mL
1 1/2 cups	Milk	375 mL

1. Cook manicotti conventionally according to package directions until al dente (tender but firm). Drain.

2. Meanwhile, beat ricotta cheese with mozzarella and Parmesan until smooth. Beat in eggs, basil, oregano and a pinch each of salt and pepper. Stuff manicotti shells with equal amounts of cheese filling. Arrange in a single layer in an 12 x 8 inch (3 L) microwavable dish.

3. To make sauce, combine butter, onion and mushrooms in a 4 cup (1 L) glass measure. Microwave, uncovered, at High (100%) for 2 to 4 minutes or until mushrooms are softened. Blend in flour, chicken stock mix, salt and pepper. Microwave, uncovered, at High (100%) for 30 seconds. Gradually whisk in Milk until smooth. Microwave, uncovered, at High (100%) for 4 to 6 minutes or until mixture comes to a boil and thickens. Whisk once or twice during cooking. Season to taste with salt and pepper.

4. Pour over manicotti. Cover with vented plastic wrap and microwave at Medium-High (70%) for 12 to 16 minutes or until heated throughout and cheese filling is firm. Rotate dish, as necessary, during cooking. Let stand, covered, for 5 to 10 minutes before serving.

Serves 4.

SPAGHETTI WITH CRISPY BACON AND CHEESE SAUCE

The hot red pepper flakes add a little heat to this quick pasta dish. Serve with a salad and you have a meal in less than 30 minutes.

1 lb.	spaghetti	500 g
1/2 lb.	lean bacon, diced	250 g
1	onion, chopped	1
2	cloves garlic, minced	2
1/4 tsp.	hot red pepper flakes	1 mL
3 tbsp.	flour	45 mL
1 1/2 cups	Milk	375 mL
1/2 cup	whipping cream	125 mL
2	eggs	2
1 cup	grated Parmesan cheese	250 mL
2 tbsp.	chopped fresh parsley	30 mL
	salt and pepper	

1. Time the conventional cooking of the spaghetti to coincide with the cooking of the sauce. Cook according to package directions until al dente (tender but firm). Drain.

2. In a 12 cup (3 L) microwavable casserole, place bacon pieces. Cover with paper towel and microwave at High (100%) for 5 to 7 minutes or until crisp. With a slotted spoon, transfer bacon to paper towel to drain. Discard all but 3 tbsp. (45 mL) bacon fat.

3. Stir onion, garlic and hot red pepper flakes into fat. Microwave, uncovered, at High (100%) for 2 to 3 minutes or until onion is tender. Blend in flour and microwave at High (100%) for 30 seconds. Gradually whisk in Milk and cream until smooth. Cover and microwave at High (100%) for 6 to 8 minutes or until mixture comes to a boil and thickens. Whisk twice during cooking.

4. Beat eggs lightly in a large serving bowl (the eggs will cook from the heat of the spaghetti and sauce). Drain spaghetti well and toss with eggs, sauce, cheese and parsley. Sprinkle top with reserved bacon. Season to taste with salt and pepper.

Serves 4 to 6.

COUNTRY STYLE SPAGHETTI

The secret is in the sausages, which add a piquant and spicy flavour to the sauce.

1 lb.	spaghetti	500 g
2 tbsp.	vegetable oil	30 mL
2	cloves garlic, minced	2
1	onion, chopped	1
1/4 tsp.	hot red pepper flakes, optional	1 mL
1 lb.	sausages (breakfast or sweet Italian) removed from casings and crumbled	500 g
2 tbsp.	flour	30 mL
2 1/2 cups	Milk	625 mL
1/2 tsp.	salt	2 mL
1/2 tsp.	pepper	2 mL
1/4 tsp.	nutmeg	1 mL
1/4 cup	chopped pimento or sweet red pepper	50 mL
1/2 cup	grated Parmesan cheese	125 mL
3 tbsp.	chopped fresh parsley	45 mL

1. Time the conventional cooking of the spaghetti to coincide with the cooking of the sauce. Cook according to package directions until al dente (tender but firm). Drain.

2. Combine oil, garlic, onion and hot red pepper flakes in an 8 cup (2 L) glass measure or microwavable casserole. Microwave, uncovered, at High (100%) for 3 to 4 minutes or until softened.

3. Add sausage meat and break up with a fork. Microwave, uncovered, at High (100%) for 5 to 7 minutes or until it loses its pink colour. Drain off fat.

4. Blend in flour and microwave, uncovered, at High (100%) for 30 seconds. Gradually stir in Milk until smooth. Add salt, pepper, nutmeg and pimento. Microwave, uncovered, at High (100%) for 6 to 8 minutes or until mixture comes to a boil. Stir 2 or 3 times during cooking. Reduce to Medium (50%) and continue to microwave for 5 minutes. Season to taste with salt and pepper.

5. Toss drained spaghetti with sauce, cheese and parsley.

Serves 4 to 6.

FETTUCCINE WITH CHICKEN AND VEGETABLES

This creamy chicken and vegetable sauce is quick and easy to prepare. Any combination of vegetables works well but a chunkier mix of broccoli, baby carrots and cauliflower is recommended.

1 lb.	dried fettuccine or medium egg noodles (green or regular noodles)	500 g
1/3 cup	butter	75 mL
1 lb.	boneless chicken breasts, cut into 2 x 3/4 inch (5 x 2 cm) strips	500 g
3 tbsp.	flour	45 mL
3 cups	Milk	750 mL
1	300 g package mixed frozen vegetables, about 3 cups (750 mL)	1
1 tsp.	salt	5 mL
1/2 tsp.	pepper	2 mL
1/4 tsp.	nutmeg	1 mL
4	green onions, sliced	4
2 tbsp.	chopped fresh dill or parsley	30 mL
1/2 cup	grated Parmesan cheese	125 mL

1. Time the conventional cooking of the fettuccine to coincide with the cooking of the sauce. Cook according to package directions until al dente (tender but firm). Drain.

2. Melt 3 tbsp. (45 mL) butter in a 12 x 8 inch (3 L) microwavable dish at High (100%) for 1 minute. Stir in chicken pieces to coat with butter. Spread evenly, cover with waxed paper and microwave at Medium-High (70%) for 5 to 7 minutes or until chicken is no longer pink. Stir at least once during cooking. Let stand, covered.

3. Melt remaining butter in an 8 cup (2 L) glass measure or micro-wavable casserole, at High (100%) for 1 minute. Blend in flour and microwave at High (100%) for 30 seconds. Gradually whisk in Milk until smooth. Cover and microwave at High (100%) for 8 to 10 minutes or until mixture comes to a boil and thickens. Whisk two or three times during cooking.

4. Add chicken and vegetables, cover and microwave at High (100%) for 3 to 5 minutes or until heated through. Add salt, pepper, nutmeg, green onions and dill. Microwave at High (100%) for 1 to 3 minutes.

5. Toss drained fettuccine with sauce and cheese. Season to taste with salt and pepper.

Serves 6.

LASAGNA

There's no need to pre-cook noodles for this recipe. It calls for the regular lasagna noodles, which soften and cook in the sauce.

2 tbsp.	vegetable oil	30	mL
1	onion, chopped	1	
2	cloves garlic, minced	2	
1/4 tsp.	hot red pepper flakes	1	mL
1 lb.	lean ground beef	500	g
2 tbsp.	flour	30	mL
1 1/2 cups	Milk	375	mL
1	28 oz. (796 mL) can tomatoes	1	
2 tbsp.	tomato paste	30	mL
1 tsp.	salt	5	mL
1/2 tsp.	pepper	2	mL
2 tbsp.	chopped fresh parsley	30	mL
1/2 lb.	dried lasagna noodles (regular, uncooked)	250	g
1 lb.	ricotta cheese (or cottage cheese, well drained)	500	g
8 oz.	thinly sliced mozzarella or Swiss cheese	250	g
1/4 cup	grated Parmesan cheese	50	mL

1. In a 12 cup (3 L) microwavable casserole combine oil, onions, garlic and hot red pepper flakes. Microwave, uncovered, at High (100%) for 3 to 4 minutes or until onion is tender.

2. Crumble ground beef into dish and microwave, uncovered, at High (100%) for 4 to 6 minutes or until beef is no longer pink. Stir twice to break up lumps. Drain off fat.

3. Stir in flour and microwave at High (100%) for 1 minute. Stir in Milk, cover and microwave at High (100%) for 4 to 6 minutes or until mixture comes to a boil and thickens. Stir at least once during cooking.

4. Stir in tomatoes, mashing with a potato masher or fork, tomato paste, salt and pepper. Cover and microwave at Medium (50%) for 8 to 10 minutes, stirring at least twice during cooking. Add parsley.and season to taste with salt and pepper.

Continued on next page

LASAGNA

(Continued)

5. Spread 1/3 sauce in bottom of a 12 x 8 inch (3 L) microwavable dish. Arrange a single layer of noodles on top. Spread with half the ricotta, half the mozzarella and 1/3 more of the meat sauce. Arrange another layer of noodles on top, spread with remaining ricotta, mozzarella and meat sauce. Sprinkle with Parmesan.

6. Cover with vented plastic wrap and microwave at Medium (50%) for 35 to 40 minutes or until noodles are tender. Rotate dish twice during cooking. Let stand, covered, for 5 to 10 minutes before serving.

Serves 6 to 8.

SPICY MACARONI AND CHEESE PARMIGIANO

This is a nippy departure from traditional macaroni and cheese. Try interesting pasta shapes such as penne, rotini, cut ziti or medium shells.

1/2 lb.	dried pasta	250	g
2 tbsp.	butter	30	mL
1	onion, chopped	1	
1/4 tsp.	hot red pepper flakes	1	mL
3 tbsp.	flour	45	mL
1/2 tsp.	salt	2	mL
1/4 tsp.	pepper	1	mL
2 cups	Milk	500	mL
1 1/2 cups	grated Parmesan cheese	375	mL
1	medium sized ripe tomato, diced	1	

1. Time the conventional cooking of the pasta to coincide with the finished sauce. Cook according to package directions until al dente (tender but firm). Drain.

2. Combine butter, onion and hot red pepper flakes in an 8 cup (2 L) glass measure or microwavable casserole. Microwave, uncovered, at High (100%) for 2 to 4 minutes or until onion is tender. Blend in flour, salt and pepper and microwave, uncovered, at High (100%) for 30 seconds.

3. Gradually whisk in Milk until smooth. Microwave, uncovered, at High (100%) for 6 to 8 minutes, or until mixture comes to a boil and thickens. Whisk twice during cooking. Stir in cheese until melted, then add tomato. Season to taste with salt and pepper.

4. Toss drained pasta with sauce.

Serves 4.

RIGATONI WESTERN

This meaty pasta dish is sure to be a hit with your family.

3/4 lb.	rigatoni noodles	375	g
1 lb.	lean ground beef	500	g
1	onion, chopped	1	
2	cloves garlic, minced	2	
3 tbsp.	flour	45	mL
2 tbsp.	chili powder	30	mL
3/4 tsp.	salt	4	mL
1/4 tsp.	pepper	1	mL
1/4 tsp.	hot red pepper flakes	1	mL
1	small green pepper, diced	1	
1	small red pepper, diced	1	
1 1/2 cups	Milk	375	mL
1	19 oz. (540 mL) can tomatoes, drained	1	
3 tbsp.	chopped fresh parsley	45	mL

1. Time the conventional cooking of the pasta to coincide with the finished sauce. Cook according to package directions until al dente (tender but firm). Drain.

2. Crumble ground beef, onion and garlic in a 12 cup (3 L) microwavable casserole. Microwave, uncovered, at High (100%) for 4 to 6 minutes or until meat is no longer pink. Stir twice to break up lumps.

3. Stir flour, chili powder, salt, pepper and hot red pepper flakes into beef mixture. Microwave, uncovered, at High (100%) for 1 minute.

4. Stir in green and red peppers, Milk and tomatoes, mashing tomatoes with a potato masher or fork. Cover and microwave at High (100%) for 12 to 15 minutes or until mixture is thickened and hot. Stir twice. Season to taste with salt and pepper.

5. Toss drained pasta with sauce and parsley.

Serves 4 to 6.

SEASIDE SHELLS

Vary the seafood to your liking. The curry powder in this dish is so subtle, it really just gives it a golden hue.

1/2 lb.	medium shells	250	g
2 tbsp.	butter	30	mL
1	onion, chopped	1	
1	clove garlic, minced	1	
2 tbsp.	flour	30	mL
1 tsp.	curry powder	5	mL
1/2 tsp.	salt	2	mL
1/4 tsp.	pepper	1	mL
1 1/2 cups	Milk	375	mL
1	4.23 oz. (120 g) can crab meat, drained and flaked	1	
1	4 oz. (113 g) can medium shrimp, drained	1	
1/4 cup	sour cream	50	mL
1 tbsp.	lemon juice	15	mL
2 tbsp.	chopped fresh dill	30	mL
	grated Parmesan cheese, optional		

1. Time the conventional cooking of the shells to coincide with the cooking of the sauce. Cook according to package directions until al dente (tender but firm). Drain.

2. Combine butter, onion and garlic in an 8 cup (2 L) glass measure or microwavable casserole. Microwave, uncovered, at High (100%) for 2 to 4 minutes or until onion is softened. Blend in flour, curry, salt and pepper and microwave, uncovered, at High (100%) for 30 seconds.

3. Gradually whisk in Milk until smooth. Microwave, uncovered, at High (100%) for 4 to 6 minutes or until mixtures comes to a boil and thickens. Whisk twice during cooking.

4. Add crab meat, shrimp, sour cream, lemon juice and dill. Stir well to blend. Season to taste with salt and pepper.

5. Toss drained shells with sauce and Parmesan cheese, if desired.

Serves 4.

CREAMY VEGETABLES AND NOODLES

With a package of mixed vegetables in the freezer and noodles in the cupboard, this is a good last minute dinner.

1/2 lb.	dried medium egg noodles	250	g
2 tbsp.	butter	30	mL
1	onion, chopped	1	
2	cloves garlic, minced	2	
2 tbsp.	flour	30	mL
1/2 tsp.	salt	2	mL
1/4 tsp.	pepper	1	mL
1 1/2 cups	Milk	375	mL
1	300 g package frozen mixed vegetables	1	
1/2 cup	grated Parmesan cheese	125	mL

1. Time the conventional cooking of the noodles to coincide with the cooking of the sauce. Cook according to package directions until al dente (tender but firm). Drain.

2. Combine butter, onion and garlic in an 8 cup (2 L) glass measure or microwavable casserole. Microwave, uncovered, at High (100%) for 2 to 4 minutes or until onion is softened. Blend in flour, salt and pepper and microwave, uncovered, at High (100%) for 30 seconds.

3. Gradually whisk in Milk until smooth. Microwave, uncovered, at High (100%) for 4 to 6 minutes or until mixture comes to a boil and thickens. Whisk twice during cooking.

4. Add frozen vegetables, stirring to break up. Microwave, uncovered, at High (100%) for 4 to 6 minutes or until heated through. Stir twice during cooking. Season to taste with salt and pepper.

5. Toss drained noodles with sauce and Parmesan cheese.

Serves 4.

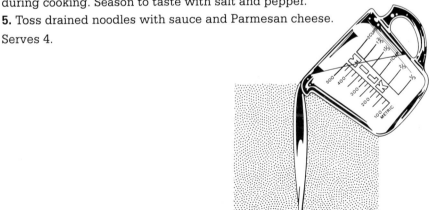

LINGUINE WITH CLAM SAUCE

This traditional pasta sauce adapts easily to the microwave.

1/2 lb.	linguine	250	g
1 tbsp.	butter	15	mL
4	green onions, chopped	4	
1	clove garlic, minced	1	
2 tbsp.	flour	30	mL
1/2 tsp.	salt	2	mL
1/4 tsp.	pepper	1	mL
1 cup	Milk	250	mL
1	5 oz. (142 g) can clams	1	
3/4 cup	clam juice plus white wine or water	175	mL
1 cup	frozen peas	250	mL
1/2 tsp.	dried tarragon	2	mL
1/2 cup	grated Parmesan cheese	125	mL

1. Time the conventional cooking of the linguine to coincide with the cooking of the sauce. Cook according to package directions until al dente (tender but firm). Drain.

2. Combine butter, green onions and garlic in an 8 cup (2 L) glass measure or microwavable casserole. Microwave, uncovered, at High (100%) for 1 to 2 minutes or until onion is softened. Blend in flour, salt and pepper and microwave, uncovered, at High (100%) for 30 seconds.

3. Gradually whisk in Milk and combined clam juice and wine or water until smooth. Microwave, uncovered, at High (100%) for 4 to 6 minutes or until mixtures comes to a boil and thickens. Whisk twice during cooking.

4. Add clams, peas and tarragon, stirring to break up peas. Microwave, uncovered, at High (100%) for 2 to 4 minutes or until peas are heated through. Stir once or twice during cooking. Season to taste with salt and pepper.

5. Toss drained linguine with sauce and Parmesan cheese.

Serves 4.

SPAGHETTINI WITH HERBED CHEESE SAUCE

Spaghettini is thin spaghetti, but you can substitute spaghetti or thin egg noodles. This is a delicious, creamy garlic and herb sauce.

1/2 lb.	spaghettini	250	g
2 tbsp.	butter	30	mL
1/3 cup	chopped green onions	75	mL
2	cloves garlic, minced	2	
1 tbsp.	flour	15	mL
1/2 tsp.	salt	2	mL
1/2 tsp.	dried basil	2	mL
1/4 tsp.	dried oregano	1	mL
1/4 tsp.	pepper	1	mL
1 cup	Milk	250	mL
1 cup	shredded mozzarella cheese	250	mL
1/2 cup	ricotta cheese	125	mL
3 tbsp.	chopped fresh parsley	45	mL

1. Time the conventional cooking of the spaghettini to coincide with the finished sauce. Cook according to package directions until al dente (tender but firm). Drain.

2. Combine butter, green onions and garlic in a 4 cup (1 L) glass measure. Microwave, uncovered, at High (100%) for 2 to 3 minutes or until softened. Blend in flour and microwave at High (100%) for 20 seconds. Stir in salt, basil, oregano and pepper.

3. Gradually whisk in Milk until smooth. Microwave, uncovered, at High (100%) for 3 to 5 minutes or until mixture comes to a boil and thickens. Whisk at least once during cooking.

4. Stir in cheeses until melted and thoroughly combined. Stir in parsley and season to taste with salt and pepper.

5. Toss drained spaghettini with sauce.

Serves 4.

PASTA AND SAUSAGE TOSS

There are a few steps to this hearty pasta dish, but it's well worth it.

1/2 lb.	rigatoni, penne or rotini pasta	250 g
1/2 lb.	Italian sausage, hot or sweet	250 g
2 tbsp.	flour	30 mL
2 tbsp.	tomato paste	30 mL
1 1/2 cups	Milk	375 mL
1/4 tsp.	salt	1 mL
1/4 tsp.	pepper	1 mL
2 tbsp.	butter	30 mL
1	onion, quartered and sliced	1
1	green pepper, quartered and sliced	1
2	cloves garlic, minced	2
1 cup	sliced fresh mushrooms	250 mL
1/2 cup	grated Parmesan cheese	125 mL

1. Time the conventional cooking of the pasta to coincide with the sauce. Cook according to package directions until al dente (tender but firm). Drain.

2. Pierce sausages in several places with tip of sharp knife. Arrange evenly on a microwave roasting rack. Cover with vented plastic wrap and microwave at Medium (50%) for 6 to 8 minutes or until cooked. Turn over partway through cooking. Uncover and let stand until cool enough to slice into 1/2 inch (1 cm) slices.

3. In an 8 cup (2 L) glass measure or microwavable casserole, whisk flour and tomato paste together until flour is incorporated and mixture is smooth. Microwave, uncovered, at High (100%) for 20 seconds. Gradually whisk in Milk until smooth. Microwave, uncovered, at High (100%) for 4 to 6 minutes or until mixture comes to boil and thickens. Whisk twice during cooking. Add salt and pepper and set aside.

4. Combine butter, onion, green pepper, garlic and mushrooms in an 8 cup (2 L) microwavable casserole. Microwave, uncovered, at High (100%) for 4 to 6 minutes or until tender. Stir at least once during cooking.

5. Stir sausages and vegetables into sauce and microwave,uncovered, at High (100%) for 1 to 3 minutes or until hot. Season to taste with salt and pepper.

6. Toss drained pasta with sauce and Parmesan cheese.

Serves 4.

WESTERN SCRAMBLED EGGS

The secret to microwave scrambled eggs is to stir often. Serve these colourful eggs with toasted English muffins or bagels.

1 tbsp.	butter	15 mL
6	eggs	6
1/2 cup	Milk	125 mL
1/2 cup	chopped cooked ham	125 mL
	salt and pepper	
1	small sized ripe tomato, chopped	1
1/2 cup	shredded white Cheddar	125 mL
	or brick cheese	

1. Melt butter in a 6 cup (1.5 L) round microwavable casserole or bowl at High (100%) for 30 to 40 seconds. Swirl butter around to coat dish. Add eggs and whisk lightly with Milk. Stir in ham.

2. Microwave, uncovered, at High (100%) for 3 to 5 minutes or until eggs are almost set but still moist. Stir every minute. Stir in chopped tomato and sprinkle with cheese. Cover and let stand for 1 minute to melt cheese. Season to taste with salt and pepper.

Serves 3 to 4.

SCRAMBLED EASTER EGG BRUNCH

An elegant way to serve scrambled eggs—spooned into patty shells and smothered in a mushroom cheese sauce.

Sauce

2 tbsp.	butter	30	mL
1 cup	sliced fresh mushrooms	250	mL
1 tbsp.	flour	15	mL
1/2 tsp.	salt	2	mL
1/4 tsp.	pepper	1	mL
1 cup	Milk	250	mL
1 cup	shredded Cheddar cheese	250	mL

Scrambled Eggs

1 tbsp.	butter	15	mL
6	eggs	6	
1/2 cup	Milk	125	mL
	salt and pepper		
6	baked patty shells (vol-au-vent)	6	

1. Combine 2 tbsp. (30 mL) butter and mushrooms in a 4 cup (1 L) glass measure. Microwave, uncovered, at High (100%) for 2 to 4 minutes or until mushrooms are tender. Blend in flour, salt and pepper and microwave, uncovered, at High (100%) for 20 seconds.

2. Gradually whisk in Milk until smooth. Microwave, uncovered, at High (100%) for 3 to 5 minutes or until mixture comes to a boil and thickens. Whisk twice during cooking. Stir in cheese until melted. Set aside.

3. Melt 1 tbsp. (15 mL) butter in a 6 cup (1.5 L) round microwavable casserole or bowl at High (100%) for 30 to 40 seconds. Swirl butter around to coat dish. Add eggs and whisk lightly with Milk.

4. Microwave, uncovered, at High (100%) for 3 to 5 minutes or until eggs are almost set but still moist. Stir every minute. Season to taste with salt and pepper.

5. To serve, fill patty shells with scrambled eggs and spoon sauce over top.

Serves 6.

EGGS BENEDICT WITH CHEESE SAUCE

This is perfect for a leisurely weekend breakfast for two or four.

1 1/2 tbsp.	butter	20 mL
1 1/2 tbsp.	flour	20 mL
3/4 tsp.	dry mustard	4 mL
1 1/4 cups	Milk	300 mL
1/4 tsp.	Tabasco sauce	1 mL
1 tbsp.	lemon juice	15 mL
1/3 cup	grated Parmesan cheese	75 mL
	salt and pepper	
4	eggs	4
2	English muffins, split	2
	butter	
2	thick slices cooked ham, cut in half	2
2 tbsp.	chopped fresh parsley	30 mL

1. Melt butter in a 4 cup (1 L) glass measure at High (100%) for 30 to 50 seconds. Blend in flour and dry mustard and microwave, uncovered, at High (100%) for 30 seconds.

2. Gradually whisk in Milk until smooth. Microwave, uncovered, at High (100%) for 3 to 5 minutes or until mixture comes to a boil and thickens. Whisk twice during cooking. Stir in Tabasco, lemon juice and cheese until cheese melts. Season to taste with salt and pepper. Cover and set aside.

3. To poach eggs, pour 2 tbsp. (30 mL) water into each of four 6 oz. (175 mL) custard cups. Arrange in a circle in microwave oven. Microwave until water boils, about 1 to 1 1/2 minutes at High (100%). Gently break eggs into boiling water. With the tip of a sharp knife gently pierce yolk and white. Cover with waxed paper and microwave at Medium (50%) for 2 to 4 minutes or until almost set. Let stand in water, covered, until needed. Eggs will continue to cook in the water. Drain.

4. Toast muffin halves, and butter lightly. Place ham slices on a microwavable plate and microwave at High (100%) for 30 to 60 seconds or until warm.

5. Place a slice of ham on each muffin half. To serve, transfer each egg with a slotted spoon onto a piece of toast. Spoon sauce over. Sprinkle with parsley. Serve one or two per person.

Serves 2 to 4.

POACHED EGGS IN SPINACH YOGURT SAUCE

Eggs can be poached in the microwave—just be sure to pierce yolks and whites to avoid bursting.

4 cups	packed fresh spinach leaves	1	L
4	eggs	4	
Sauce			
1 tbsp.	butter	15	mL
1	small onion, sliced	1	
1 tbsp.	flour	15	mL
1/2 cup	Milk	125	mL
1/2 cup	plain yogurt or sour cream	125	mL
1/2 tsp.	dried dill weed	2	mL
	salt and pepper		
4	slices of bread, toasted	4	

1. Wash spinach well and remove stems. Shake off excess moisture and place in an 8 cup (2 L) microwavable casserole or bowl. Cover with vented plastic wrap and microwave at High (100%) for 3 to 4 minutes or until cooked. Drain well, squeezing out excess moisture. Chop well. [You should have about 1/2 cup (125 mL).] Set aside.

2. To poach eggs, pour 2 tbsp. (30 mL) water into each of four 6 oz. (175 mL) custard cups. Arrange in a circle in microwave oven. Microwave until water boils, about 1 to 1 1/2 minutes at High (100%). Gently break eggs into boiling water. With the tip of a sharp knife gently pierce yolk and white. Cover with waxed paper and microwave at Medium (50%) for 2 to 4 minutes or until eggs are almost set. If you hear a popping sound, stop cooking and check progress. It may be necessary to rotate or lower the power level to avoid overcooking. Let stand in water, covered, until needed. Eggs will continue to cook in the water.

3. Combine butter and onion in a 4 cup (1 L) glass measure and microwave at High (100%) for 2 to 3 minutes until softened. Blend in flour and microwave at High (100%) for 20 seconds.

4. Gradually whisk in Milk until smooth. Microwave, uncovered, at High (100%) for 1 to 3 minutes or until mixture comes to a boil and thickens. Whisk once during cooking. Stir in chopped spinach, yogurt, dill weed and salt and pepper to taste.

5. To serve, transfer each egg with a slotted spoon onto a piece of toast. Spoon sauce over.

Serves 4.

MUSHROOM AND RED PEPPER FRITTATA

This classic Italian egg dish is similar to a baked omelet. As a main course, serve with salad and crusty rolls.

2 tbsp.	butter	30 mL
1	small onion, chopped	1
1	clove garlic, minced	1
1 cup	sliced fresh mushrooms	250 mL
1	small red pepper, diced	1
1 tbsp.	flour	15 mL
2 tbsp.	chopped fresh parsley	30 mL
4	eggs	4
3/4 cup	Milk	175 mL
1/2 tsp.	salt	2 mL
1/4 tsp.	pepper	1 mL
1 cup	shredded Cheddar cheese	250 mL
1/4 cup	fresh breadcrumbs	50 mL
2 tbsp.	grated Parmesan cheese	30 mL

1. Combine butter, onion, garlic, mushrooms and red pepper in an 8 cup (2 L) glass measure. Microwave, uncovered, at High (100%) for 4 to 6 minutes or until vegetables are softened. Stir once during cooking.

2. Blend in flour and microwave at High (100%) for 30 seconds. Add parsley and set aside.

3. Whisk eggs and Milk together. Add vegetables and remaining ingredients except Parmesan cheese. Pour into a 9 inch (23 cm) microwavable quiche dish or deep dish glass pie plate.

4. Microwave, uncovered, at Medium (50%) for 12 to 15 minutes or until almost set in the centre. Rotate dish, as necessary, during cooking.

5. Sprinkle with Parmesan cheese and let stand directly on countertop for 10 to 15 minutes before serving.

Serves 4.

ASPARAGUS RAREBIT

When you want a light dinner or luncheon, spoon a cheese sauce over fresh asparagus and toasted English muffins.

1/2 lb.	fresh asparagus	250	g
1/4 cup	water	50	mL
3 tbsp.	butter	45	mL
3 tbsp.	flour	45	mL
1/2 tsp.	salt	2	mL
1/2 tsp.	dry mustard	2	mL
1/4 tsp.	pepper	1	mL
1 1/2 cups	Milk	375	mL
1 cup	shredded Cheddar cheese	250	mL
1 tsp.	Worcestershire sauce	5	mL
4	English muffins, split and toasted	4	

1. Rinse asparagus under cold running water. Snap off and discard woody stem ends. Cut in half crosswise. Arrange stalks at outer edges of a shallow microwavable dish in a single layer. Place tips in centre of dish. Pour water over and cover with vented plastic wrap. Microwave at High (100%) for 2 to 4 minutes or until tender crisp. Let stand, covered, while making sauce.

2. Melt butter in a 4 cup (1 L) glass measure at High (100%) for 45 to 60 seconds. Blend in flour, salt, dry mustard and pepper and microwave, uncovered, at High (100%) for 30 seconds.

3. Gradually whisk in Milk until smooth. Microwave, uncovered, at High (100%) for 4 to 6 minutes or until mixture comes to a boil and thickens. Whisk twice during cooking. Stir in cheese until melted. Add Worcestershire.

4. To serve, divide asparagus between muffin halves and spoon sauce over top.

Serves 4.

CHICKEN, LEEK AND MUSHROOM QUICHE

This quiche has a light breadcrumb base. If you prefer, a baked pastry crust made in a 9 inch (23 cm) quiche dish or deep dish glass pie plate can be used. Fill and bake as below.

Base

2 tsp.	softened butter	10	mL
2 tbsp.	dry breadcrumbs	30	mL
or 1	9 inch (23 cm) baked pastry shell	or 1	

Filling

2 tbsp.	butter	30	mL
1 cup	sliced leeks, white part only	250	mL
1 cup	sliced fresh mushrooms	250	mL
1 tbsp.	flour	15	mL
1 cup	diced, cooked chicken	250	mL
1 cup	Milk	250	mL
4	eggs	4	
1/2 tsp.	dried tarragon	2	mL
1/4 tsp.	salt	1	mL
1/4 tsp.	pepper	1	mL

1. Generously rub sides and bottom of a 9 inch (23 cm) microwavable quiche dish, deep dish pie plate or round cake dish with butter. Add breadcrumbs and shake back and forth to coat the sides and bottom. Refrigerate while making filling.

2. Combine butter, leeks and mushrooms in a 4 cup (1 L) microwavable casserole. Microwave, uncovered, at High (100%) for 3 to 4 minutes or until vegetables are tender. Blend in flour and microwave, uncovered, at High (100%) for 30 seconds. Stir in chicken and set aside.

3. Microwave Milk in a 1 cup (250 mL) glass measure at High (100%) for 1 1/2 to 2 minutes or until hot but not boiling.

4. Whisk together eggs and Milk, tarragon, salt and pepper. Spoon chicken mixture over refrigerated base. Pour egg mixture evenly over chicken and microwave, uncovered, at Medium (50%) for 12 to 16 minutes or until almost set in the centre. Rotate dish, as necessary, during cooking.

5. Let stand on countertop for 10 minutes before serving.

Serves 4 to 6.

BACON, CHEESE AND ONION TART

Quiches such as this one make a delightful brunch, lunch dish or serve as a light supper with a salad.

Base

2 tsp.	softened butter	10	mL
2 tbsp.	dry breadcrumbs	30	mL
or 1	9 inch (23 cm) baked pastry shell	or 1	

Filling

4	slices bacon, diced	4	
2	medium onions, sliced	2	
1 tbsp.	flour	15	mL
1 cup	shredded Swiss cheese	250	mL
1 cup	Milk	250	mL
4	eggs	4	
1/4 tsp.	dried oregano	1	mL
1/4 tsp.	dried thyme	1	mL
1/4 tsp.	salt	1	mL
1/4 tsp.	pepper	1	mL

1. Generously rub sides and bottom of a 9 inch (23 cm) microwavable quiche dish, deep dish pie plate or round cake dish with butter. Add breadcrumbs and shake back and forth to coat the sides and bottom. Refrigerate while making filling.

2. Place bacon in a 6 cup (1.5 L) microwavable casserole. Cover with paper towel and microwave at High (100%) for 3 to 4 minutes or until bacon is almost crisp. Transfer with a slotted spoon to paper towel. Discard all but 1 tbsp. (15 mL) bacon fat. Stir onions into bacon fat and microwave, uncovered, at High (100%) for 3 to 4 minutes or until onions are softened. Stir partway through cooking. Blend in flour and microwave, uncovered, at High (100%) for 30 seconds. Spread bacon, onions and cheese evenly in refrigerated base.

3. Microwave Milk in a 1 cup (250 mL) glass measure at High (100%) for 1 1/2 to 2 minutes or until hot but not boiling.

4. Whisk together eggs and Milk, oregano, thyme, salt and pepper. Pour evenly over bacon, onions and cheese. Microwave, uncovered, at Medium (50%) for 10 to 14 minutes or until almost set in the centre. Rotate, as necessary, during cooking.

5. Let stand on countertop for 10 minutes before serving.

Serves 4.

VEGETABLES

Broccoli and Cauliflower
with Almonds

Scalloped Potatoes with
Cheese and Herbs

Vegetables

This section features some interesting combinations such as cabbage and potatoes, celery and leeks, sweet potato and rutabaga, as well as vegetables that star on their own. Recipes for fresh, frozen and seasonal vegetables are all included, so you can enjoy them year round.

Potatoes get a new lease on life in Creamy Scalloped Potatoes, baked in one-sixth the time of conventional cooking, and Double Baked Potatoes, almost a quick light meal in themselves.

BROCCOLI AND CAULIFLOWER WITH ALMONDS

This vegetable dish uses frozen broccoli and cauliflower. If you prefer, use 1 1/2 cups (375 mL) each of cooked fresh vegetables.

1/4 cup	butter	50 mL
1/4 cup	flour	50 mL
1 tsp.	curry powder	5 mL
2 1/2 cups	Milk	625 mL
1 tbsp.	apricot chutney or jam	15 mL
	salt and pepper	
1 cup	shredded Swiss cheese	250 mL
1	300 g package frozen broccoli, defrosted*	1
1	300 g package frozen cauliflower, defrosted*	1

Topping

1/4 cup	butter	50 mL
1 1/2 cups	fresh breadcrumbs, toasted	375 mL
1/2 cup	sliced almonds, toasted	125 mL

1. Melt butter in a 12 cup (3 L) microwavable casserole at High (100%) for 1 to 1 1/2 minutes. Blend in flour and curry powder and microwave at High (100%) for 30 seconds.

2. Gradually whisk in Milk and chutney until smooth. Microwave, uncovered, at High (100%) for 6 to 9 minutes or until mixture comes to a boil and thickens. Whisk twice during cooking. Season to taste with salt and pepper. Stir in cheese until melted. Add broccoli and cauliflower.

3. To make topping, melt butter in a 4 cup (1 L) microwavable casserole at High (100%) for 1 minute. Stir in breadcrumbs and almonds. Sprinkle over broccoli and cauliflower and microwave at Medium-High (70%) for 4 to 6 minutes or until hot and bubbling.

Serves 4 to 6.

*Defrost vegetables in the microwave according to package directions.

DOUBLE BAKED POTATOES

Stuffed potatoes can be made in one third of the conventional cooking time.

4	large baking potatoes	4
2 tbsp.	butter	30 mL
1	onion, chopped	1
1	clove garlic, minced	1
3/4 cup	Milk	175 mL
	salt and pepper	
1/4 tsp.	nutmeg	1 mL
1/2 lb.	bacon, cooked crisp and crumbled*	250 g
1 cup	shredded Cheddar cheese	250 mL
2 tbsp.	chopped fresh chives or green onions	30 mL
1 tbsp.	butter, melted	15 mL

1. Scrub potatoes and dry well. Pierce each with fork in several places. Arrange in a circle, on double thickness of paper towel, about 2 inches (5 cm) apart. Microwave, uncovered, at High (100%) for 15 to 20 minutes or until almost tender. Turn over partway through cooking. Let stand, uncovered.

2. Combine butter, onion and garlic in a 4 cup (1 L) glass measure or microwavable casserole. Microwave, uncovered, at High (100%) for 2 to 3 minutes or until softened. Stir in Milk, salt and pepper to taste, and nutmeg. Microwave, uncovered, at High (100%) for 1 to 2 minutes or until hot.

3. Cut off top third of potatoes. Scoop out potato pulp, leaving 1/4 inch (5 mm) shell. Beat pulp until smooth. Stir in Milk mixture, bacon, cheese and chives.

4. Spoon or pipe potato mixture back into potato skins. Brush with melted butter and place on a microwavable plate. Microwave, uncovered, at Medium (50%) for 8 to 10 minutes or until heated through.

Serves 4.

* To microwave bacon, arrange half the amount evenly on microwave roasting rack. Cover with paper towel and microwave at High (100%) until crisp. Change paper towel as necessary to absorb excess fat. Repeat with remaining strips. Crumble when cool.

BAKED WINTER SQUASH RING

This can be assembled ahead and refrigerated; cook just before serving. For a festive meal, fill centre of ring with Brussels sprouts and garnish with cherry tomatoes and parsley.

2 lbs.	butternut, hubbard or acorn squash	1	kg
1 lb.	carrots	500	g
1/2 cup	water	125	mL
3 tbsp.	packed brown sugar	45	mL
1/2 tsp.	salt	2	mL
1/2 tsp.	cinnamon	2	mL
1/2 tsp.	ground ginger	2	mL
1/4 tsp.	nutmeg	1	mL
1/4 tsp.	pepper	1	mL
5	eggs	5	
1 cup	Milk	250	mL
1 cup	fresh breadcrumbs	250	mL

1. Pierce squash in several places with tip of a sharp knife. Place on paper towel and microwave at High (100%) for 8 to 12 minutes or until tender. Turn over once during cooking. Cooking time will vary with size and type of squash. Let stand until cool enough to handle. Cut squash in half, remove seeds and scoop out enough pulp for 2 cups (500 mL).

2. While squash is cooking, peel and dice carrots. Place in a 6 cup (1.5 L) microwavable casserole with water. Cover and microwave at High (100%) for 10 to 12 minutes or until very tender. Stir or shake dish once during cooking. Let stand, covered, for 10 minutes, then drain and purée in food processor. Measure out 1 cup (250 mL).

3. In a large bowl combine squash, carrot, brown sugar, salt, cinnamon, ginger, nutmeg and pepper. Beat eggs with Milk and add to squash. Stir in breadcrumbs.

4. Butter a 6 cup (1.5 L) microwavable ring mould. Spoon mixture into mould and smooth until even. Cover with waxed paper and microwave at High (100%) for 10 to 14 minutes or until firm and set. A toothpick inserted in several places should come out clean. Rotate dish, as necessary, during cooking.

5. Let stand, uncovered, for 10 minutes. Run a knife around edge of mould and invert onto serving platter.

Serves 6 to 8.

MASHED POTATOES WITH MUSHROOMS

Adding mushrooms and Cheddar cheese to an everyday favourite has turned it into something very special. This also reheats well if you plan to make it ahead.

2 lbs.	baking potatoes	1	kg
1/4 cup	water	50	mL
2 tbsp.	butter	30	mL
1	onion, chopped	1	
1	clove garlic, minced	1	
1	12 oz. (340 g) package frozen mushrooms or 2 cups (500 mL) sliced fresh mushrooms	1	
1/2 tsp.	dried tarragon	2	mL
3/4 cup	Milk	175	mL
1 tsp.	salt	5	mL
1/4 tsp.	pepper	1	mL
3/4 cup	shredded Cheddar cheese	175	mL
2 tbsp.	butter	30	mL
2 tbsp.	chopped fresh chives or green onions	30	mL

1. Peel potatoes and cut into 2 inch (5 cm) pieces. Place in a 12 cup (3 L) microwavable casserole with water. Cover with vented plastic wrap or casserole lid and microwave at High (100%) for 12 to 16 minutes or until potatoes are tender. Stir occasionally. Let stand, covered.

2. Combine butter, onion, garlic and mushrooms in an 8 cup (2 L) glass measure or microwavable casserole. Microwave, uncovered, at High (100%) for 6 to 9 minutes or until tender. Stir at least once during cooking.

3. Stir tarragon into Milk. Microwave at High (100%) for 2 to 4 minutes or until Milk comes to a boil.

4. Drain potatoes and mash. Beat Milk mixture into potatoes and season with salt and pepper. Stir in cheese and butter until cheese melts. Garnish with chives or green onions.

Serves 4 to 6.

SWEET POTATO AND RUTABAGA BAKE

This colourful vegetable casserole goes nicely with turkey, chicken, ham or pork and it's just right for a small Christmas or Thanksgiving dinner.

1	large sweet potato, about 3/4 1b. (375 g)	1
2 cups	large diced rutabaga	500 mL
1/2 cup	Milk	125 mL
2 tbsp.	butter, divided	30 mL
1	egg	1
1/2 tsp.	grated orange peel	2 mL
1 tbsp.	orange juice	15 mL
	mace or nutmeg, salt and pepper	
12	toasted pecan halves*	12

1. Pierce sweet potato in several places with a sharp knife. Place on paper towel and microwave, uncovered, at High (100%) for 5 to 8 minutes or until tender. Let stand 10 minutes, uncovered.

2. Meanwhile combine rutabaga, Milk and 1 tbsp. (15 mL) of the butter in a 10 cup (2.5 L) microwavable casserole. Cover and microwave at High (100%) for 6 to 8 minutes or until rutabaga is tender. Let stand, covered, for 5 minutes.

3. Starting at low speed, beat rutabaga with electric mixer until almost smooth. Peel sweet potato and add potato to rutabaga, beating until smooth.

4. Mix together egg, orange peel and orange juice just until blended; add mixture to vegetables. Then add mace, salt and pepper to taste.

5. Transfer to a 4 cup (1 L) soufflé dish or microwavable casserole. Spread with remaining 1 tbsp. (15 mL) butter and score top attractively with a fork. Arrange pecans in a circle on top. Microwave, uncovered, at High (100%) for 5 to 8 minutes or until heated through and slightly pulled away from edge of dish. Let stand briefly.

Serves 4.

* **To toast pecan halves,** spread out on a shallow microwavable dish such as a glass pie plate. Microwave, uncovered, at High (100%) for 1 to 3 minutes or until lightly toasted and fragrant. Stir or shake dish to prevent scorching.

ASPARAGUS MIMOSA WITH MOCK HOLLANDAISE

This Hollandaise Sauce is lower in butter and eggs than conventional recipes, but still has a rich smooth texture.

2	hard-cooked eggs, shelled	2	
1/3 cup	butter, divided	75	mL
1 tbsp.	flour	15	mL
1/2 cup	Milk	125	mL
2 tbsp.	lemon juice	30	mL
1	egg yolk	1	
	cayenne, salt and pepper		
1 lb.	asparagus	500	g
1/4 cup	water	50	mL

1. Hard cook the eggs conventionally, then make the sauce before cooking the asparagus. Separate egg whites and yolks from hard cooked eggs, chop and set aside.

2. Melt 1 tbsp. (15 mL) of the butter in a 2 cup (500 mL) glass measure at High (100%) for 20 to 30 seconds. Blend in flour and microwave, uncovered, at High (100%) for 20 seconds. Gradually whisk in Milk until smooth. Microwave, uncovered, at High (100%) for 2 to 4 minutes or until mixture comes to a boil and thickens. Whisk once.

3. Combine lemon juice and egg yolk and whisk into sauce. Microwave, uncovered, at Medium (50%) for 1 to 3 minutes or until thick. Whisk at least twice. Add cayenne, salt and pepper to taste. Whisk in remaining butter, about 1 1/2 tsp. (7 mL) at a time. Make sure each addition is absorbed before adding more. Cover Hollandaise Sauce loosely with paper towel and set aside.

4. Snap off and discard tough stem ends of asparagus. Rinse well in cold water. Arrange in a shallow microwavable dish just large enough to hold them in a single layer, with stalks towards outer edges of dish and tips in the centre. Add water, cover with vented plastic wrap and microwave at High (100%) for 5 to 7 minutes or until tender.

5. Drain immediately and transfer to warmed serving dish. Arrange strips of chopped, hard-cooked egg yolk and white attractively over asparagus. Pour Hollandaise Sauce between strips of egg or serve separately.

Serves 4.

SAVORY CABBAGE AND POTATO CASSEROLE

This dish, of British origin, has the unusual name of Bubble and Squeak, as well as many other variations. It was a customary way to use up vegetables left over from Sunday dinner and is often tastier than the first serving. You can cook and combine the vegetables ahead, ready to pop into the microwave at the last minute.

4 cups	coarsely chopped cabbage	1 L
	salt	
1 lb.	potatoes (about 2 large), peeled and cut into 2 inch (5 cm) pieces	500 g
3	slices bacon, chopped	3
1/2 cup	Milk	125 mL
2 tbsp.	butter, divided	30 mL
1/2 tsp.	dried savory	2 mL
	pepper	

1. Combine cabbage and 1/4 cup (50 mL) water in a 10 cup (2.5 L) microwavable casserole or bowl. Season lightly with salt and cover with vented plastic wrap or lid. Microwave at High (100%) for 6 to 8 minutes or until tender. Stir twice during cooking. Drain in colander, cover with a small plate and weight down (an unopened can or a jar filled with water works well). Set aside.

2. Combine potatoes and 1/4 cup (50 mL) water in same 10 cup (2.5 L) casserole or bowl. Cover and microwave at High (100%) for 6 to 8 minutes or until tender. Stir gently partway through cooking. Drain and set aside, covered.

3. Place bacon in a 9 inch (23 cm) shallow microwavable dish between double thickness of paper towel. Microwave at High (100%) for 1 to 2 minutes or until partially crisp. Set aside.

4. Mash potatoes with Milk and 1 tbsp. (15 mL) of the butter until smooth. Stir in cabbage, savory and pepper to taste. Spread mixture in a well buttered 9 inch (23 cm) shallow microwavable dish and spread remaining 1 tbsp. (15 mL) butter evenly over the top. Score attractively with a fork and sprinkle with bacon.

5. Microwave, uncovered, at High (100%) for 5 to 7 minutes or until heated through and slightly pulled away from edges of dish. Let stand a few minutes before serving.

Serves 4 to 6.

CHEESE STUFFED MUSHROOMS

You can make the filling, stuff the mushrooms and refrigerate, ahead of time. They take only a few minutes in the microwave. Serve as a tasty accompaniment to any meat or poultry dish.

8	large mushrooms, about 2 1/2 inches (6 cm) in diameter	8
3 tbsp.	butter, divided	45 mL
2	cloves garlic, minced	2
1 tbsp.	flour	15 mL
1 cup	mini-croutons*	250 mL
1 cup	shredded Cheddar cheese	250 mL
1 tbsp.	chopped fresh parsley	15 mL
1/2 cup	Milk	125 mL
1/2 tsp.	Worcestershire sauce	2 mL
	salt and pepper	
2 tbsp.	fine dry breadcrumbs	30 mL

1. Wipe mushrooms with damp paper towels, scoop out centres and finely chop centres and stems. Combine chopped mushrooms, 2 tbsp. (30 mL) butter and garlic in a 6 cup (1.5 L) microwavable casserole. Microwave, uncovered, at High (100%) for 2 to 3 minutes or until mushrooms are softened. Sprinkle with flour, blend well and microwave, uncovered, at High (100%) for 1 minute. Stir in croutons, cheese, parsley, Milk, Worcesterhire sauce and salt and pepper to taste. Mix well and let stand, uncovered for 10 minutes.

2. Meanwhile, in a 9 inch (23 cm) shallow microwavable dish, microwave remaining 1 tbsp. (15 mL) butter at High (100%) for 20 to 30 seconds.

3. Fill mushroom caps with cheese mixture and arrange in a circle in melted butter in shallow dish. Sprinkle with breadcrumbs. (If making ahead, cover with paper towel and refrigerate.)

4. Microwave, covered with paper towel, at High (100%) for 3 to 5 minutes or until caps are tender. Let stand, briefly.

Serves 4.

* Use purchased croutons or melt 1 tbsp. (15 mL) butter in a shallow microwavable dish such as a glass pie plate at High (100%) for 20 to 30 seconds. Stir in 1 cup (250 mL) of 1/4 inch (5 mm) diced bread cubes, coating with butter. Microwave, uncovered, at High (100%) for 3 to 5 minutes or until lightly golden and quite dry. Stir or shake dish often to prevent scorching. Let stand, until cool. (They will continue to crisp up during standing time.)

SCALLOPED POTATOES WITH CHEESE AND HERBS

If you like a crusty or browned top, run briefly under preheated broiler after standing time.

3 tbsp.	butter	45 mL
2	onions, chopped	2
2	cloves garlic, minced	2
3 tbsp.	flour	45 mL
1 1/2 cups	Milk	375 mL
1/2 tsp.	salt	2 mL
1/4 tsp.	dried rosemary	1 mL
1/4 tsp.	dried basil	1 mL
1/4 tsp.	dried oregano	1 mL
1/4 tsp.	pepper	1 mL
4	medium potatoes, peeled and thinly sliced	4
1 cup	shredded Swiss cheese	250 mL

1. Combine butter, onions and garlic in an 8 cup (2 L) round microwavable casserole. Microwave, uncovered, at High (100%) for 3 to 4 minutes or until onions are softened.

2. Blend in flour and microwave at High (100%) for 30 seconds. Gradually whisk in Milk until smooth. Microwave, uncovered, at High (100%) for 4 to 6 minutes or until mixture comes to a boil and thickens. Whisk twice during cooking. Add salt, rosemary, basil, oregano and pepper.

3. Add potatoes, mixing gently to cover with sauce. Cover and microwave at High (100%) for 12 to 16 minutes or until fork tender. Stir gently once during cooking. Sprinkle with cheese and let stand, covered, for 10 to 15 minutes. Broil, if desired until golden brown.

Serves 4 to 6.

BROCCOLI WITH
SAUCE BELLE CRÈME

Belle Crème is a tangy soft surface-ripened cheese that melts very smoothly. Canadian Camembert can be substituted, if desired.

1 tbsp.	butter	15	mL
2	medium onions, cut into wedges	2	
3 cups	broccoli florets	750	mL
2 tbsp.	water	30	mL
4 oz.	Belle Crème cheese or Canadian Camembert, chilled	125	g
1 tbsp.	flour	15	mL
1/2 cup	Milk	125	mL
	cayenne, nutmeg, salt and pepper		

1. Melt butter in a 9 inch (23 cm) round shallow microwavable dish at High (100%) for 20 to 30 seconds. Toss onion wedges in butter to coat.

2. Arrange broccoli between onion wedges with stalks towards outer edge of dish. Sprinkle with water and cover with vented plastic wrap. Microwave at High (100%) for 4 to 6 minutes or until broccoli is tender. Let stand, covered, while making sauce.

3. Remove and discard rind from cheese; cut into cubes. Toss cheese with flour in a 2 cup (500 mL) glass measure. Microwave, uncovered, at Medium (50%) for 1 minute or until melted.

4. Whisk in Milk, a pinch each of cayenne, nutmeg, salt and pepper. Microwave, uncovered, at High (100%) for 2 to 3 minutes or until mixture comes to a boil and thickens.

5. To serve, drain vegetables and pour Cheese Sauce over all. Serve immediately.

Serves 4.

CAULIFLOWER WITH CHEESE SAUCE

As simple as this sounds and is, a whole cauliflower makes an impressive presentation. A good standing time is important for complete cooking and provides the ideal time to make the sauce.

1	medium cauliflower	1
2 tbsp.	butter	30 mL
3	green onions, chopped	3
2 tbsp.	flour	30 mL
1/2 tsp.	salt	2 mL
1/2 tsp.	dry mustard	2 mL
1/4 tsp.	pepper	1 mL
1 cup	Milk	250 mL
3/4 cup	shredded sharp Cheddar cheese	175 mL

1. Trim leaves off whole cauliflower and remove as much of the core as possible. Wash well and place in a shallow microwavable dish such as a glass pie plate. Sprinkle with 1 tbsp. (15 mL) water and cover with vented plastic wrap. Microwave at High (100%) for 10 to 15 minutes or until almost tender when pierced with a sharp knife. Rotate dish, as necessary, during cooking. Let stand, covered, for 10 to 15 minutes to complete cooking.

2. Combine butter and green onions in a 4 cup (1 L) glass measure. Microwave, uncovered, at High (100%) for 1 to 2 minutes or until onions are softened. Blend in flour, salt, dry mustard and pepper; microwave, uncovered, at High (100%) for 30 seconds.

3. Gradually whisk in Milk until smooth. Microwave, uncovered, at High (100%) for 3 to 5 minutes or until mixture comes to a boil and thickens. Whisk once or twice during cooking. Stir in cheese until melted.

4. To serve, drain cauliflower and pour cheese sauce over all.

Serves 6.

MIXED VEGETABLES ITALIAN STYLE

This vegetable dish will add an attractive dash of colour to any dinner.
Be sure to use firm but ripe tomatoes.

2	medium, firm, ripe tomatoes	2
1/2	green pepper	1/2
1/2	red pepper	1/2
1	small onion	1
3 tbsp.	butter, divided	45 mL
2	cloves garlic, minced	2
1/2 tsp.	dried oregano	2 mL
2 cups	cauliflower florets	500 mL
Sauce		
4 tsp.	butter	20 mL
4 tsp.	flour	20 mL
1 cup	Milk	250 mL
pinch	nutmeg	pinch
	salt and pepper	
1/2 cup	grated Parmesan cheese	125 mL

1. Peel tomatoes and cut each into 6 wedges. Remove and discard seeds.
Cut green and red peppers into 1/2 inch (1 cm) strips, then cut strips
diagonally into diamond shapes. Cut onion into 6 wedges and separate
layers. Set aside.

2. In a 10 inch (25 cm) shallow microwavable dish, melt 2 tbsp. (30 mL)
of the butter at High (100%) for 1 minute or until it sizzles. Stir in
peppers, onion, garlic and oregano. Microwave, uncovered, at High
(100%) for 2 to 3 minutes or until softened.

3. Add cauliflower to outer edges of dish, pushing pepper mixture
towards the centre. Cover with vented plastic wrap and microwave at
High (100%) for 3 to 4 minutes or until tender crisp.

4. Melt remaining 1 tbsp. (15 mL) butter. Arrange tomato wedges, cut
side down, between cauliflower and brush with melted butter. Cover
and microwave at High (100%) for 2 to 4 minutes or until tender. Let
stand, covered, while making sauce.

Continued on next page

MIXED VEGETABLES ITALIAN STYLE
(Continued)

5. Melt butter in a 2 cup (500 mL) glass measure at High (100%) for 30 to 40 seconds. Blend in flour and microwave, uncovered, at High (100%) for 20 seconds. Gradually whisk in Milk until smooth. Add nutmeg and salt and pepper to taste. Microwave, uncovered, at High (100%) for 3 to 5 minutes or until mixture comes to a boil and thickens. Whisk once during cooking. Stir in cheese until melted.

6. Pour about 1/3 of the sauce over the vegetables. Pass remaining sauce separately.

Serves 4.

CREAMED PEAS WITH MUSHROOMS

For best results use tiny, button mushrooms no more than an inch (2.5 cm) in diameter.

1	350 g package frozen baby peas	1
2 tbsp.	butter, divided	30 mL
1 cup	small whole mushrooms	250 mL
1 tbsp.	flour	15 mL
3/4 cup	Milk	175 mL
	nutmeg, cayenne, salt and pepper	
1 tbsp.	chopped fresh dill	15 mL
1/2 tsp.	grated lemon peel	2 mL

1. Combine frozen peas and 1/4 cup (50 mL) water in a 6 cup (1.5 L) microwavable casserole. Cover with vented plastic wrap and microwave at High (100%) for 4 to 6 minutes or until cooked through. Stir partway. Let stand, covered.

2. In a 6 cup (1.5 L) microwavable casserole, microwave 1 tbsp. (15 mL) of the butter at High (100%) for 1 minute or until sizzling. Stir in mushrooms, coating well with butter. Microwave, uncovered, at High (100%) for 2 to 3 minutes or until tender. Set aside.

3. Melt remaining 1 tbsp. (15 mL) butter in a 2 cup (500 mL) glass measure at High (100%) for 30 to 40 seconds. Blend in flour and microwave, uncovered, at High (100%) for 20 seconds.

4. Gradually whisk in Milk until smooth. Season with a pinch each of nutmeg, cayenne, salt and pepper. Microwave, uncovered, at High (100%) for 3 to 5 minutes or until mixture comes to a boil and thickens. Stir at least once during cooking. Stir in dill and lemon peel.

5. Drain peas, add to mushrooms and mix gently to combine. Stir in sauce and microwave, uncovered, at High (100%) for 1 to 3 minutes or until heated through. Serve immediately.

Serves 4.

CREAMY VEGETABLE CASSEROLE

This is an attractive way to serve a variety of vegetables. Julienne the carrots and zucchini so that they will fit neatly around the cauliflower to make an attractive display. If you can't find a small cauliflower, trim off the outer florets of a larger one and reserve for another time.

1 cup	julienned carrots	250 mL
1	small cauliflower, about 5 inches (12 cm) in diameter	1
3 tbsp.	butter, divided	45 mL
1 cup	julienned zucchini	250 mL
2 tbsp.	flour	30 mL
1 1/4 cups	Milk	300 mL
dash	Tabasco sauce	dash
	mace, salt and pepper	
1 cup	shredded white Cheddar cheese	250 mL

1. In a small microwavable bowl, combine carrots and 2 tbsp. (30 mL) water. Cover with vented plastic wrap and microwave at High (100%) for 3 to 4 minutes or until tender crisp. Let stand, covered.

2. Trim leaves off whole cauliflower and remove as much of the core as possible, but leave intact. Place in centre of large, buttered microwavable plate or platter. Spread 1 tbsp. (15 mL) of the butter over cauliflower and cover with vented plastic wrap. Microwave at High (100%) for 3 to 5 minutes or until tender crisp. Drain carrots and arrange around cauliflower in small bunches alternately with zucchini. Cover and microwave at High (100%) for 3 to 5 minutes. Let stand, covered.

3. Melt remaining 2 tbsp. (30 mL) butter in a 4 cup (1 L) glass measure at High (100%) for 40 to 60 seconds. Blend in flour and microwave at High (100%) for 30 seconds. Gradually whisk in Milk until smooth. Add Tabasco, a pinch each of mace, salt and pepper. Microwave, uncovered, at High (100%) for 3 to 5 minutes or until mixture comes to a boil and thickens. Stir at least once during cooking. Stir in cheese until melted.

4. Pour any accumulated liquid off vegetables and pour sauce over cauliflower and a little around carrots and zucchini. Microwave, uncovered, at High (100%) for 1 minute or until heated through.

Serves 4.

DESSERTS

Chocolate Banana Trifle

Easy Raisin Rice Pudding

Desserts

Making Milk-based desserts in the microwave is so easy, even the most timid cook will be won over.

Some of the recipes in this section combine conventionally baked pastry crust or tart shells with a microwaved filling. But if time becomes important, an alternate crumb crust can often be baked in the microwave in minutes.

The rich flavour of maple, caramel, mocha, chocolate and orange are just some of the taste sensations you'll find in these recipes celebrating the nutritious versatility of Milk desserts.

STREUSEL BAKED APPLES WITH VANILLA SAUCE

Serve this warming dessert straight from the microwave. Make the
Vanilla Sauce first, then bake the apples while eating dinner.

Vanilla Sauce

2 tbsp.	sugar	30 mL
1 tbsp.	cornstarch	15 mL
3/4 cup	Milk	175 mL
1	egg, lightly beaten	1
1/2 tsp.	vanilla	2 mL

Apples

1/3 cup	packed brown sugar	75 mL
1/2 tsp.	cinnamon	2 mL
1/4 tsp.	nutmeg	1 mL
1 tbsp.	chilled butter	15 mL
3	large cooking apples	3
2 tbsp.	raisins	30 mL

1. To make sauce, combine sugar and cornstarch in a 2 cup (500 mL)
glass measure. Gradually whisk in Milk until smooth. Microwave,
uncovered, at High (100%) for 2 to 4 minutes or until mixture comes to a
boil and thickens. Whisk at least once during cooking.

2. Stir a small amount of hot sauce into lightly beaten egg. Pour warmed
egg back into sauce, whisking constantly.

3. Microwave, uncovered, at Medium (50%) for 30 seconds to 1 minute or
until thickened. Stir in vanilla. Cover Vanilla Sauce to keep warm.

4. Combine brown sugar, cinnamon and nutmeg. Cut in butter until
mixture is crumbly.

5. Halve and core apples. Pierce skin of apples in several places with the
tip of a sharp knife. Arrange cut side up in a single layer in a shallow
microwavable dish, such as a large pie plate or quiche dish. Place 1 tsp.
(5 mL) raisins in hollow of each apple. Spoon about 1 tbsp. (15 mL)
brown sugar mixture over top of each apple half.

6. Microwave, uncovered, at High (100%) for 5 to 8 minutes or until
apples are tender. Rotate dish, as necessary, during cooking. Cooking
time will vary with type and size of apple.

7. To serve, place an apple half in each serving dish. Spoon the cooking
liquid over the apples, then top with Vanilla Sauce. Serve warm.

Serves 6.

CRUNCHY CARAMEL MOUSSE

This heavenly dessert is worth the effort. Allow enough time for preparation and be careful when handling the hot sugar mixture.

1 1/2 cups	sugar	375	mL
2/3 cup	water, divided	150	mL
1	envelope unflavoured gelatin	1	
3 tbsp.	rum or water	45	mL
3	egg yolks	3	
1 1/2 cups	Milk	375	mL
1 tsp.	vanilla	5	mL
2 cups	whipping cream	500	mL
2 oz.	semi-sweet or bittersweet chocolate	60	g
2	Crispy Crunch bars, crushed (45 g each)	2	

1. Combine sugar and 1/3 cup (75 mL) of the water in a heavy, deep 8 cup (2 L) microwavable bowl. Stir until blended. Microwave, uncovered, at High (100%) for 10 to 12 minutes or until sugar turns a deep caramel colour. Do not stir and do not allow to burn. Carefully remove bowl with pot holders and standing back, add remaining 1/3 cup (75 mL) water. Stir until smooth. Set aside.

2. Sprinkle gelatin over rum or water in a small microwavable bowl or custard cup and let stand 5 minutes to soften.

3. Meanwhile, measure Milk into a 2 cup (500 mL) glass measure and microwave at High (100%) for 3 to 4 minutes or until hot. Set aside.

4. Microwave gelatin mixture at High (100%) for 30 to 60 seconds or until gelatin is completely dissolved.

5. Place egg yolks in an 8 cup (2 L) glass measure or microwavable bowl. Gradually whisk hot Milk into egg yolks. Whisk in caramel and gelatin. Microwave, uncovered, at High (100%) for 3 to 4 minutes or until mixture thickens slightly. Whisk every minute and do not allow to boil or egg yolks may curdle.

6. Add vanilla and cool over a large bowl filled with ice and water. Stir until mixture is cool but not set.

Continued on next page

CRUNCHY CARAMEL MOUSSE

(Continued)

7. Meanwhile, melt chocolate in a small microwavable dish at Medium (50%) for 2 to 3 minutes, stirring to help melt chocolate. Prepare a large serving bowl by drizzling half the chocolate around the bottom and up the sides. Sprinkle with half the crushed chocolate bars. Set aside.

8. Whip cream until firm, then fold 2/3 into the cool caramel mixture. Pour into serving bowl. Refrigerate mousse and extra cream for one hour.

9. Decorate top of mousse with reserved cream and drizzle with remaining chocolate. Sprinkle with remaining crushed chocolate bars. Chill two hours or until firm.

Serves 6 to 8.

COCONUT CRUNCH CUSTARDS

These individually baked custards are topped with a coconut mixture and then broiled to caramelize the topping. They will cook at different rates, so remove those that are done and re-position remainder to avoid overcooking.

2 cups	Milk	500 mL
5	eggs	5
1/3 cup	sugar	75 mL
1 1/2 tsp.	vanilla	7 mL
1/2 cup	dessicated or flaked coconut	125 mL
2 tbsp.	packed brown sugar	30 mL
1 tbsp.	butter	15 mL
1/4 tsp.	cinnamon	1 mL

1. Measure Milk into a 2 cup (500 mL) glass measure and microwave at High (100%) for 3 to 4 minutes or until hot, but not boiling.

2. While Milk is heating, whisk eggs and sugar together until light and frothy. Add vanilla, then gradually whisk in hot Milk.

3. Divide mixture between six 6 oz. (175 mL) custard cups. Cover with waxed paper and microwave at Medium (50%) for 6 to 9 minutes or until set and knife inserted near centre comes out clean. Re-position the dishes once or twice as necessary. Remove as they are cooked. Let stand, uncovered, and cool to room temperature.

4. Combine coconut, brown sugar, butter and cinnamon. Sprinkle evenly over top of each custard. Broil under preheated broiler until golden brown, about 1 minute. Watch carefully to avoid burning.

Serves 6.

CLASSIC CREME CARAMEL

This wonderful dessert can be made in one quarter of the conventional time and without the fuss of a water bath. Serve at room temperature or make ahead to serve chilled.

1 cup	sugar, divided	250	mL
2 tbsp.	water	30	mL
2 1/2 cups	Milk	625	mL
3	egg yolks	3	
3	eggs	3	
1 tsp.	vanilla	5	mL

1. Combine 1/2 cup (125 mL) of the sugar and water in a heavy, round 5 cup (1.25 L) microwavable dish, such as a soufflé dish. Microwave, uncovered, at High (100%) for 4 to 6 minutes or until sugar caramelizes to a dark golden brown. Watch carefully to avoid burning and do not stir. Remove dish with pot holders and rotate dish so that caramel coats the sides as well as the bottom. Set aside to cool and harden, about 15 minutes.

2. Measure Milk into a 4 cup (1 L) glass measure and microwave at High (100%) for 3 to 4 minutes or until hot, but not boiling.

3. While Milk is heating, whisk egg yolks, eggs and remaining 1/2 cup (125 mL) sugar together until light and frothy. Add vanilla, then gradually whisk in hot Milk.

4. Pour mixture over cooled caramel. Cover with casserole lid or waxed paper and microwave at Medium (50%) for 8 to 12 minutes or until set and knife inserted near centre comes out clean. Rotate dish, during cooking, as necessary. Let stand, covered, and cool to room temperature. Serve warm or chill until serving time.

5. To serve, place a serving plate with a rim, over dish and quickly turn crème caramel out of dish.

Serves 4 to 6.

VARIATION:

Orange Crème Caramel: Thinly peel half an orange with potato peeler. Add peel to Milk before heating. Strain before whisking into eggs. Add 1 tbsp. (15 mL) orange liqueur along with vanilla.

DESSERT FONDUES

For a casual ending to a meal, serve a festive fondue with fresh fruit, cubes of pound cake or plain cookies for dipping. You can either keep the sauce warm over a candle flame or return it to the microwave as needed.

Chocolate Fondue
You can vary the liqueur to your preference.

1	350 g package semi-sweet chocolate pieces, about 2 cups (500 mL)	1
1 cup	Milk	250 mL
2 tbsp.	coffee liqueur	30 mL
1/2 tsp.	vanilla	2 mL

1. Combine chocolate chips and Milk in a 4 cup (1 L) glass measure or microwavable bowl. Microwave, uncovered, at High (100%) for 2 to 3 minutes or until partially melted. Stir to complete melting. Stir in liqueur and vanilla.

Makes 2 cups (500 mL).

Butterscotch Fondue
This is creamy and delicious. If you enjoy rum and butter, add 1 tbsp. (15 mL) rum or 1 tsp. (5 mL) rum extract to finished sauce.

1/2 cup	packed dark brown sugar	125 mL
1 tbsp.	flour	15 mL
pinch	salt	pinch
1 cup	Milk	250 mL
2 tbsp.	butter	30 mL
1 tsp.	vanilla	5 mL

1. Combine sugar, flour and salt in a 4 cup (1 L) glass measure or micro-wavable bowl. Gradually whisk in Milk until smooth.
2. Microwave, uncovered, at High (100%) for 3 to 4 minutes or until mixture comes to a boil and thickens. Whisk at least twice during cooking.
3. Stir in butter until melted, then add vanilla.

Makes 1 1/3 cups (325 mL).

Continued on next page

DESSERT FONDUES
(Continued)

Creamy Vanilla Fondue
This versatile fondue goes well with a wide variety of flavours.

1/2 cup	sugar	125 mL
2 tsp.	cornstarch	10 mL
1 cup	Milk	250 mL
1/4 cup	butter	50 mL
1 1/2 tsp.	vanilla	7 mL

1. Combine sugar and cornstarch in a 4 cup (1 L) glass measure or micro-wavable bowl. Gradually whisk in Milk until smooth.

2. Microwave, uncovered, at High (100%) for 2 to 3 minutes or until mixture comes to a boil and thickens slightly. Whisk at least once during cooking.

3. Stir in butter until melted, then add vanilla.

Makes 1 1/2 cups (375 mL).

Dippers: sliced bananas, apples, peaches, melon balls, orange segments, strawberries, cherries, grapes or cubes of pound cake or plain cookies.

CHOCOLATE BANANA TRIFLE

A chocolate-lovers delight! This looks spectacular in individual servings or can be made in a large bowl and garnished with candied violets.

3 1/2 cups	Milk	875 mL
1 tbsp.	instant coffee granules	15 mL
1/2 cup	sugar	125 mL
1/3 cup	cornstarch	75 mL
2	eggs	2
6 oz.	semi-sweet chocolate, chopped	175 g
2 tbsp.	unsweetened cocoa powder	30 mL
1 tsp.	vanilla	5 mL
3	bananas	3
1	200 g package chocolate wafer cookies	1
1 cup	whipping cream	250 mL
2 tbsp.	sugar	30 mL

1. Combine Milk and coffee granules in an 8 cup (2 L) glass measure. Microwave at High (100%) for 8 to 10 minutes or until Milk comes to a boil. Stir 2 or 3 times.

2. Meanwhile combine 1/2 cup (125 mL) sugar with cornstarch and beat in eggs.

3. Reserve 2 tbsp. (30 mL) chopped chocolate for the garnish. Add remaining chocolate and cocoa to hot Milk and stir until chocolate melts. Whisk cornstarch egg mixture into Milk. Microwave at Medium (50%) for 4 to 6 minutes or until mixture thickens. Whisk often. Add vanilla.

4. Slice bananas. Break up chocolate cookies coarsely and place 1/3 of them in the bottom of a 6 cup (1.5 L) bowl. Cover with 1/2 the custard. Top with 1/2 the sliced bananas. Layer cookies, custard and bananas again and top with a layer of cookies.

5. Whip cream with 2 tbsp. (30 mL) sugar and spread over final layer of cookies. Sprinkle with reserved chocolate.

6. This can be eaten immediately, however cookies will soften and become more cake-like if trifle is refrigerated a few hours.

Serves 6 to 8.

CARROT CAKE WITH CREAM CHEESE FROSTING

A large 12 cup (3 L) microwave bundt pan is needed for this size of cake. Alternately, divide batter into 2 round 9 inch (23 cm) glass cake dishes. Bake one at a time, dividing cooking time accordingly.

3/4 cup	butter, softened	175 mL
1 cup	packed brown sugar	250 mL
3	eggs	3
2 cups	all-purpose flour	500 mL
2 tsp.	baking powder	10 mL
1 1/2 tsp.	cinnamon	7 mL
1/4 tsp.	nutmeg	1 mL
1 cup	Milk	250 mL
2 1/2 cups	grated carrots	625 mL
1/2 cup	raisins	125 mL
1/2 cup	chopped pecans	125 mL
1/4 cup	chopped candied orange peel, optional	50 mL
Icing		
6 oz.	cream cheese, softened	175 g
1/4 cup	butter	50 mL
1 tbsp.	Milk	15 mL
2 cups	sifted icing sugar	500 mL

1. Cream butter until light. Gradually beat in sugar. Add eggs one at a time, beating well after each addition.

2. Combine flour, baking powder, cinnamon and nutmeg. Stir into butter mixture alternately with Milk, beginning and ending with dry ingredients. Stir in carrots, raisins, pecans and candied peel, if using.

3. Spoon into a lightly buttered 12 cup (3 L) microwave bundt pan. Microwave, uncovered, at Medium (50%) for 8 minutes. Rotate pan and continue microwaving at High (100%) for 4 to 8 minutes or until surface is nearly dry and a toothpick inserted in several places comes out clean. Touch any moist spots with your finger—if the cake underneath is dry, it is done.

4. Let stand directly on counter for 10 minutes. Run a thin spatula around edges of cake. Invert onto serving plate and cool completely before icing.

5. For icing, beat cream cheese until smooth. Beat in butter. Blend in Milk. Stir in icing sugar until frosting is smooth and spreadable. Ice cake and sprinkle with toasted coconut, if desired.

VANILLA PUDDING PLUS

Milk puddings are so easy to make in the microwave—no worry about scorched pots or burnt Milk. Use a large container such as an 8 cup (2 L) glass measure to avoid boilovers and a whisk to prevent lumps. Whisk every two minutes to ensure a smooth pudding.

1/2 cup	sugar	125 mL
3 tbsp.	cornstarch	45 mL
pinch	salt	pinch
2 1/4 cups	Milk	550 mL
1 1/2 tsp.	vanilla	7 mL

1. Combine sugar, cornstarch and salt in an 8 cup (2 L) glass measure. Gradually whisk in Milk until smooth.

2. Microwave, uncovered, at High (100%) for 6 to 8 minutes or until mixture comes to a boil and thickens. Whisk every 2 minutes.

3. Stir in vanilla. Cool slightly, then pour into serving dishes. To prevent a skin from forming, place a piece of plastic wrap or waxed paper directly on surface of pudding. Chill until set, about 2 hours.

Makes 3 cups (750 mL); six 1/2 cup (125 mL) servings.

VARIATIONS:

Coconut Pudding: Stir 1/2 cup (125 mL) flaked coconut into cooked pudding along with vanilla.

Banana Pudding: Stir 1 or 2 sliced, ripe bananas into finished vanilla pudding.

Orange Pudding: To cooked vanilla pudding, add 1 tbsp. (15 mL) grated orange peel and 1/2 tsp. (2 mL) orange extract.

Lemon Pudding: To cooked vanilla pudding, add 1 tbsp. (15 mL) grated lemon peel and 1/2 tsp. (2 mL) lemon extract.

Chocolate Pudding: Increase sugar to 2/3 cup (150 mL) and add 1/4 cup (50 mL) unsweetened cocoa powder to cornstarch and salt before adding 2 cups (500 mL) Milk.

Mocha Pudding: To chocolate pudding, add 1 tbsp. (15 mL) instant coffee granules to sugar, cornstarch, salt and cocoa mixture before adding the 2 cups (500 mL) Milk.

BANANA SCOTCH–ER–OO PUDDING

The meringue on this pudding will set very nicely in the microwave. However, if you want a lightly browned top, run under a preheated broiler after microwaving.

1	4 serving size package butterscotch or vanilla pudding and pie filling	1
2	eggs, separated	2
2 1/2 cups	Milk	625 mL
2	large ripe bananas, sliced	2
1/4 cup	sugar	50 mL

1. Whisk pudding mix, egg yolks and Milk in an 8 cup (2 L) glass measure until smooth. Microwave, uncovered, at High (100%) for 5 to 8 minutes or until mixture comes to a boil and thickens. Whisk every 2 minutes. Cover surface of pudding with plastic wrap and let cool to room temperature.

2. Alternately layer pudding and banana slices in a 4 cup (1 L) round microwavable casserole or bowl, beginning and ending with pudding.

3. Beat egg whites until frothy. Gradually beat in sugar until stiff peaks form. Spread evenly over pudding, sealing edges well. Microwave, uncovered, at Medium (50%) for 3 to 4 minutes or until meringue is set. Brown lightly under preheated broiler, if desired. Serve warm.

Serves 6 to 8.

PEANUT BUTTER PUDDING

A favourite with kids of all ages and so easy to make.

1/2 cup	sugar	125 mL
2 tbsp.	cornstarch	30 mL
pinch	salt	pinch
2 cups	Milk	500 mL
1/2 cup	peanut butter	125 mL
1 tsp.	vanilla	5 mL
	chopped peanuts, optional	

1. Combine sugar, cornstarch and salt in an 8 cup (2 L) glass measure. Gradually whisk in Milk until smooth.

2. Microwave, uncovered, at High (100%) for 5 to 8 minutes or until mixture comes to a boil and thickens. Whisk every 2 minutes.

3. Stir in peanut butter until melted, then add vanilla. Cool slightly, then pour into serving dishes. To prevent a skin from forming, place a piece of plastic wrap or waxed paper directly on surface of pudding. Chill until set, about 2 hours.

Makes 3 cups (750 mL); six 1/2 cup (125 mL) servings.

CHILLY LIME SOUFFLE

The perfect dessert after a rich meal or when the temperature soars.
Make early in the day or the day before.

1 1/2 cups	Milk	375 mL
2	envelopes unflavoured gelatin	2
4	eggs, separated	4
1/4 cup	sugar	50 mL
1	6 1/4 oz. (177 mL) can frozen limeade concentrate, thawed	1
1/4 cup	lime juice	50 mL
	green food colouring	
1 tsp.	cream of tartar	5 mL
3/4 cup	whipping cream	175 mL
	lime slices	

1. Fasten a 2 inch (5 cm) foil collar around a 5 cup (1.25 L) soufflé dish.

2. Measure Milk into a 4 cup (1 L) glass measure. Sprinkle gelatin over Milk and let stand 5 minutes to soften. Stir mixture and microwave at High (100%) for 3 to 4 minutes or until gelatin is completely dissolved. Stir often to help the granules dissolve. Set aside to cool.

3. In a large bowl, beat together egg yolks and sugar until thick. Add limeade concentrate, lime juice and a few drops of green food colouring. Stir in Milk and chill until mixture mounds on a spoon.

4. Beat egg whites with cream of tartar until stiff but not dry. Whip cream to soft peaks. Gently fold both into lime mixture.

5. Turn into prepared soufflé dish and chill until set, several hours or overnight.

6. To serve, remove collar and garnish with fresh lime slices.

Serves 8.

EASY STEAMED CHRISTMAS PUDDINGS

The microwave steams these individual Christmas puddings in 12 minutes or less and without the hassle of a water bath. Make just before serving, as they dry out quickly. Serve with Custard Sauce (recipe below).

1 1/2 cups	vanilla wafer crumbs	375	mL
1/2 cup	all purpose flour	125	mL
1/2 tsp.	baking soda	2	mL
1/2 tsp.	cinnamon	2	mL
1/2 tsp.	nutmeg	2	mL
1/4 tsp.	salt	1	mL
1/4 cup	shortening	50	mL
1/2 cup	packed dark brown sugar	125	mL
1	egg	1	
1/2 cup	Milk	125	mL
1/2 cup	slivered almonds	125	mL
1/2 cup	chopped glacé cherries (red or green or half of each)	125	mL

Custard Sauce

2 tbsp.	sugar	30	mL
1 tbsp.	cornstarch	15	mL
3/4 cup	Milk	175	mL
1	egg, lightly beaten	1	
1/2 tsp.	vanilla	2	mL

1. In a small bowl combine wafer crumbs, flour, baking soda, cinnamon, nutmeg and salt.

2. In a larger bowl, cream shortening and sugar until light. Beat in egg until smooth. Add dry ingredients to egg mixture alternately with Milk until blended. Stir in almonds and cherries.

3. Spoon into six lightly buttered 6 oz. (175 mL) custard cups. Arrange in a circle in microwave oven, allowing about 1 inch (2.5 cm) between each cup. Cover with waxed paper and microwave at Medium (50%) for 8 to 12 minutes or until toothpick inserted in several places comes out clean. Rotate, as necessary during cooking. Uncover and let stand on countertop for 10 to 15 minutes.

Continued on next page

EASY STEAMED CHRISTMAS PUDDINGS

(Continued)

4. To make sauce, combine sugar and cornstarch in a 2 cup (500 mL) glass measure. Gradually whisk in Milk until smooth. Microwave, uncovered, at High (100%) for 2 to 4 minutes or until mixture comes to a boil and thickens. Whisk at least once during cooking.

5. Stir a small amount of hot sauce into lightly beaten egg. Pour warmed egg back into sauce, whisking constantly. Microwave, uncovered, at Medium (50%) for 30 seconds to 1 minute or until thickened. Stir in vanilla. Cover to keep warm.

6. Run a thin spatula or knife along edges of each pudding. Unmould and serve warm with Custard Sauce. If not serving immediately, let cool completely then wrap well in plastic wrap. Reheat puddings and sauce at Medium (50%), just until warm.

Serves 6.

MOCHA SWIRL CHEESECAKE

This no-bake cheesecake is attractive, rich and delicious.

Crust

1/4 cup	butter	50	mL
1 cup	graham crumbs	250	mL
1/2 cup	chopped pecans	125	mL

Filling

1 cup	Milk	250	mL
1	envelope unflavoured gelatin	1	
1 tbsp.	instant coffee granules	15	mL
1	8 oz. (250 g) package cream cheese	1	
1/3 cup	sugar	75	mL
2	eggs, separated	2	
1/2 tsp.	vanilla	2	mL
2 oz.	semi-sweet chocolate	60	g
2 tbsp.	coffee liqueur	30	mL
2 tbsp.	sugar	30	mL

1. Melt butter in either a 9 inch (23 cm) microwavable quiche dish, round baking dish or 9 1/2 inch (24 cm) deep dish glass pie plate. [You need a dish large enough to hold 6 cups (1.5 L) volume. A regular 9 inch (23 cm) pie plate only holds 4 cups (1 L).] Microwave at High (100%) for 1 to 1 1/2 minutes. Stir in crumbs until evenly coated with butter. Press onto bottom and side of dish. Microwave at High (100%) for 2 to 3 minutes or until firm. Rotate plate, if necessary, during cooking. Set aside.

2. Measure Milk in a 2 cup (500 mL) glass measure. Sprinkle gelatin over Milk and let stand for 5 minutes to soften. Microwave at High (100%) for 1 to 2 minutes or until gelatin is dissolved. Stir in instant coffee granules until dissolved. If necessary, microwave at High (100%) for 30 to 60 seconds or until coffee dissolves. Set aside to cool.

3. Beat cream cheese with 1/3 cup (75 mL) sugar until light. Beat in egg yolks, one at a time, then vanilla. Gradually beat in gelatin mixture until smooth. Chill until mixture mounds slightly on a spoon, but is not set.

4. Combine chocolate and liqueur in a 2 cup (500 mL) glass measure or bowl. Microwave at Medium (50%) for 1 to 2 minutes or until almost melted. Stir to finish melting. Cool slightly.

Continued on next page

MOCHA SWIRL CHEESECAKE

(Continued)

5. Beat egg whites until frothy. Gradually beat in 2 tbsp. (30 mL) sugar until stiff but not dry. Fold gently into gelatin mixture.

6. Divide this mixture into 2 bowls. Add chocolate mixture to one bowl and blend well. Then spoon both mixtures into baked crust, alternating spoonfuls. Swirl with a knife to give a marbled effect. Chill until set, several hours or overnight.

Serves 8.

MANDARIN CHEESECAKE

This is a light, refreshing cheesecake with the delectable combination of chocolate and orange. If you can't find the pressed cottage cheese, drain regular cottage cheese well and blend until smooth in a food processor.

Crust

1/4 cup	butter	50	mL
1 1/2 cups	chocolate wafer or chocolate graham crumbs	375	mL

Filling

1	10 oz. (284 mL) can mandarin oranges	1	
1	envelope unflavoured gelatin	1	
1	egg, separated	1	
1/3 cup	sugar	75	mL
1/2 cup	Milk	125	mL
1 tbsp.	grated orange peel	15	mL
1/2 tsp.	vanilla	2	mL
2 tbsp.	sugar	30	mL
1 lb.	pressed cottage cheese (10% b.f.)	500	g
1 oz.	semi-sweet chocolate, optional	30	g

1. Melt butter in either a 9 inch (23 cm) microwavable quiche dish, round baking dish or 9 1/2 inch (24 cm) deep dish glass pie plate. [You need a dish large enough to hold 6 cups (1.5 L) volume. A regular 9 inch (23 cm) pie plate only holds 4 cups (1 L).] Microwave at High (100%) for 1 to 1 1/2 minutes. Stir in crumbs until evenly coated with butter. Press onto bottom and side of dish. Microwave at High (100%) for 2 to 3 minutes, or until firm. Rotate, if necessary, during cooking. Set aside.

2. Drain juice from mandarin segments into a small dish. Sprinkle gelatin over juice and let stand for 5 minutes to soften. Reserve mandarin segments for garnish.

3. Whisk together egg yolk, 1/3 cup (75 mL) sugar and Milk in a medium microwavable bowl. Whisk in softened gelatin. Microwave, uncovered, at High (100%) for 2 to 3 minutes or until gelatin is dissolved and mixture is hot but not boiling. Whisk every minute. Stir in orange peel and vanilla and set aside to cool.

Continued on next page

MANDARIN CHEESECAKE

(Continued)

4. Beat egg white until frothy. Gradually beat in remaining 2 tbsp. (30 mL) sugar until stiff but not dry. Set aside.

5. Without cleaning beaters, beat cottage cheese in a large bowl until smooth. Beat in gelatin mixture. Gently fold in beaten egg white. Spoon into baked crust. Chill until set, several hours or overnight.

6. Garnish with reserved mandarin segments. If desired, melt chocolate in a small microwavable dish at Medium (50%) for 1 to 2 minutes. Stir to help melting. Drizzle over top in an attractive pattern. Chill until chocolate is set.

Serves 8.

BANANA SPLIT PIE

With all the ingredients of a banana split, this is a hit with kids and adults alike.

Crust

1/4 cup	butter	50	mL
1 1/4 cups	graham crumbs	300	mL

Filling

1	6 serving size package banana pudding and pie filling	1	
2 cups	Milk	500	mL
2	ripe bananas	2	
1 cup	whipping cream	250	mL
	maraschino cherries, chopped nuts		
	Regal Chocolate Sauce, page 48		

1. Melt butter in a 9 inch (23 cm) glass pie plate at High (100%) for 1 to 1-1/2 minutes. Stir in crumbs until evenly coated with butter. Press onto bottom and side of dish. Microwave at High (100%) for 2 to 3 minutes or until firm. Rotate dish, if necessary, during cooking. Set aside to cool.

2. Whisk pudding mix and Milk together in an 8 cup (2 L) glass measure until smooth. Microwave, uncovered, at High (100%) for 5 to 8 minutes, or until mixture comes to a boil and thickens. Whisk every 2 minutes. Cool slightly and spoon into pie shell. Chill well.

3. Just before serving, slice bananas and arrange on top of filling. Whip cream until stiff and spoon or pipe on top of bananas. Garnish with cherries, nuts and chocolate sauce, as desired.

Serves 6 to 8.

PEANUT BUTTER PIE

This is a triple-layered pie—peanut butter, then custard and finally a meringue top. Bake the pie crust conventionally and brown the meringue under the broiler.

1	9 inch (23 cm) baked pie crust	1
3/4 cup	crunchy or smooth peanut butter	175 mL
1/4 cup	honey	50 mL
1/4 cup	sugar	50 mL
1/4 cup	cornstarch	50 mL
2 cups	Milk	500 mL
2	eggs, separated	2
1 tsp.	vanilla	5 mL
1/4 tsp.	cinnamon	1 mL
1/4 tsp.	nutmeg	1 mL
2 tbsp.	sugar	30 mL

1. Combine peanut butter and honey until smooth. Spread on bottom of baked pie crust. Set aside.

2. Combine 1/4 cup (50 mL) sugar and cornstarch in an 8 cup (2 L) glass measure. Gradually whisk in Milk until smooth. Microwave, uncovered, at High (100%) for 5 to 8 minutes or until mixture comes to a boil and thickens. Whisk every 2 minutes. Add a little of the hot mixture to egg yolks. Return warmed yolks to measure, whisking constantly. Microwave at Medium (50%) for 1 minute or until thickened. Add vanilla, cinnamon and nutmeg. Cool slightly, then spoon on top of peanut butter.

3. Beat egg whites until frothy. Gradually add 2 tbsp. (30 mL) sugar and beat until stiff but not dry. Spread meringue over pie, sealing to the edges of crust. Broil under preheated broiler until meringue is lightly browned. Watch carefully to avoid burning.

4. Chill until set.

Serves 6 to 8.

GRASSHOPPER PIE

Named for its bright green colour, this chilled mint filling is in a chocolate crumb base.

Crust

1/4 cup	butter	50	mL
1 1/4 cups	chocolate wafer or chocolate graham crumbs	300	mL

Filling

1/2 cup	sugar	125	mL
1	envelope unflavoured gelatin	1	
3/4 cup	Milk	175	mL
2	eggs, separated	2	
1/4 cup	green Crème de Menthe liqueur	50	mL
2 tbsp.	sugar	30	mL
1 cup	whipping cream	250	mL
	green food colouring		

1. Melt butter in a 9 inch (23 cm) microwavable pie plate, at High (100%) for 1 to 1 1/2 minutes. Stir in crumbs until evenly coated with butter. Press onto bottom and side of dish. Microwave at High (100%) for 2 to 3 minutes or until firm. Rotate plate, if necessary, during cooking. Set aside.

2. In a large microwavable bowl or casserole combine 1/2 cup (125 mL) sugar and gelatin. Stir in Milk and microwave, uncovered, at High (100%) for 2 to 4 minutes or until hot but not boiling. Stir to help dissolve gelatin.

3. Add a little of hot mixture to egg yolks. Return warmed yolks to bowl, whisking constantly. Microwave at Medium (50%) for 1 minute or until thickened. Stir in liqueur and chill until slightly thickened but not set.

4. Beat egg whites until frothy. Gradually beat in 2 tbsp. (30 mL) sugar and beat until stiff but not dry. Whip 1/2 cup (125 mL) whipping cream until soft peaks form.

5. Tint gelatin mixture with green food colouring. Fold beaten egg whites and cream into mixture. Spoon into baked crust and chill until set.

6. To serve, whip remaining cream and spoon or pipe on top of pie.

Serves 6 to 8.

MANDARIN CREAM PIE

This simple no-bake pie is ideal to make and serve in hot weather.

Crust

1/4 cup	butter	50	mL
1 1/4 cups	graham crumbs	300	mL
1/4 tsp.	ground ginger	1	mL

Filling

3/4 cup	Milk	175	mL
1 cup	sour cream	250	mL
1 tbsp.	grated orange peel	15	mL
1	4 serving size package instant vanilla pudding	1	
1	10 oz. (284 mL) can mandarin orange segments, well drained	1	

1. Microwave butter in a 9 inch (23 cm) microwavable pie plate at High (100%) for 1 to 1 1/2 minutes. Stir in crumbs until evenly coated with butter. Reserve 2 tbsp. (30 mL) for garnish. Press remaining onto bottom and side of dish. Microwave at High (100%) for 2 to 3 minutes or until firm. Rotate plate, if necessary, during cooking. Set aside.

2. Beat Milk, sour cream, orange peel and pudding mix until thick. Pour into crust and chill until firm.

3. To serve, arrange mandarin orange segments on top of pie and sprinkle with reserved crumbs.

Serves 6 to 8.

MAPLE SUGAR CHIFFON PIE

A delectably light pie with a crunchy candy garnish. Make your favourite pie shell, but be sure it is big enough to hold a large volume. Bake pie shell conventionally.

1	10 inch (25 cm) or 9 1/2 inch (24 cm) deep dish baked pie shell	1	
2 tbsp.	cornstarch	30	mL
2 cups	Milk	500	mL
1/2 cup	maple syrup	125	mL
1	envelope unflavoured gelatin	1	
1/4 cup	water	50	mL
3	eggs, separated	3	
1 tsp.	vanilla	5	mL
2 tbsp.	maple syrup	30	mL
Maple Nut Crunch			
2 tbsp.	butter	30	mL
1/2 cup	chopped pecans or walnuts	125	mL
1/3 cup	maple syrup	75	mL

1. Place cornstarch in an 8 cup (2 L) glass measure or large microwavable bowl. Gradually whisk in Milk, then maple syrup until smooth. Microwave, uncovered, at High (100%) for 6 to 8 minutes or until mixture comes to a boil and thickens. Whisk every 2 minutes.

2. Meanwhile, sprinkle gelatin over water to soften. Set aside.

3. Stir a small amount of hot custard into egg yolks. Pour warmed yolks back into custard, whisking constantly. Microwave, uncovered, at Medium (50%) for 1 to 2 minutes or until thickened. Whisk well; do not allow to boil.

4. Stir softened gelatin into mixture until dissolved. Add vanilla and chill until thickened but not set.

5. Beat egg whites until almost stiff. Continue beating, adding 2 tbsp. (30 mL) maple syrup. Fold gently into custard and pour into baked crust. Chill until firm.

6. To make Maple Nut Crunch, combine butter and nuts in a 4 cup (1 L) glass measure. Microwave at High (100%) for 2 to 3 minutes or until boiling. Stir in maple syrup and microwave, uncovered, at High (100%) until syrup reaches hard crack stage, 300°F (150°C) on candy thermometer. Do not leave candy thermometer in microwave oven. Cooking time will be from 3 to 5 minutes. Pour immediately onto a cookie sheet. Let cool and harden. Break up into small pieces.

7. To serve, sprinkle pie with Maple Nut Crunch.

Serves 8.

COCONUT ALMOND PIE

A delicious combination of coconut and almond. Simply irresistable!

Crust

1/4 cup	butter	50	mL
1 1/4 cups	graham or vanilla wafer crumbs	300	mL

Filling

1/2 cup	sugar	125	mL
1	envelope unflavoured gelatin	1	
1/4 tsp.	salt	1	mL
1 cup	Milk	250	mL
3	eggs, separated	3	
1 tsp.	vanilla	5	mL
1/2 tsp.	almond extract	2	mL
1/4 cup	slivered almonds	50	mL
1/4 cup	flaked or shredded coconut	50	mL

1. Melt butter in either a 9 inch (23 cm) microwavable quiche dish, round baking dish or 9 1/2 inch (24 cm) deep dish glass pie plate. [You need a dish large enough to hold 6 cups (1.5 L) volume. A regular 9 inch (23 cm) pie plate only holds 4 cups (1 L).] Microwave at High (100%) for 1 to 1 1/2 minutes. Stir in crumbs until evenly coated with butter. Press onto bottom and side of dish. Microwave at High (100%) for 2 to 3 minutes or until firm. Rotate plate, if necessary, during cooking. Set aside.

2. Combine sugar, gelatin and salt in a large microwavable bowl. Gradually whisk in Milk until smooth. Microwave, uncovered, at High (100%) for 2 to 4 minutes or until hot, but not boiling. Stir to help dissolve gelatin.

3. Whisk a small amount of hot liquid into egg yolks. Pour warmed yolks back into mixture, whisking constantly. Microwave, uncovered, at Medium (50%) for 3 to 4 minutes or until slightly thickened. Whisk often and do not allow to boil.

4. Stir in vanilla and almond extract. Cool, then chill until thickened but not set.

5. Beat egg whites until stiff but not dry. Fold gently into almond mixture. Pour into baked crust and chill until set.

Continued on next page

COCONUT ALMOND PIE

(Continued)

6. Meanwhile, toast almonds in a shallow microwavable plate such as a glass pie plate at High (100%) for 4 to 6 minutes. Stir or shake dish often to prevent scorching. Toast coconut in another shallow microwavable dish at High (100%) for 3 to 4 minutes or until golden. Stir every 30 seconds and watch carefully as coconut scorches easily.

7. Sprinkle pie with almonds and coconut just before serving.

Serves 6 to 8.

CITRUS CREAM

This light cream mixture is absolutely perfect after a heavy
meal.

1	orange	1
	orange juice	
1/4 cup	lemon juice	50 mL
1	envelope unflavoured gelatin	1
1 1/2 cups	Milk	375 mL
3	eggs, separated	3
1/2 cup	sugar	125 mL
pinch	salt	pinch
2 tbsp.	sugar	30 mL

1. Grate peel from orange, set aside. Squeeze juice from orange into a
1 cup (250 mL) glass measure. Add additional orange juice to make
1/2 cup (125 mL). Add lemon juice to orange juice. Sprinkle gelatin over
juices, set aside to soften.

2. Microwave Milk in a 2 cup (500 mL) glass measure, uncovered, at
High (100%) for 2 minutes or until hot.

3. In a medium microwavable bowl, whisk egg yolks with 1/2 cup
(125 mL) sugar and salt. Gradually whisk in Milk and orange peel until
smooth. Microwave, uncovered, at High (100%) for 3 to 4 minutes or
until hot, but not boiling. Whisk often.

4. Stir gelatin mixture into Milk mixture until gelatin dissolves. Cool to
room temperature, then chill until mixture is the consistency of
unbeaten egg whites.

5. Beat egg whites until frothy. Gradually beat in remaining 2 tbsp.
(30 mL) sugar until stiff but not dry. Fold into custard mixture and pour
into a 4 cup (1 L) dish or mould. Chill until set.

Serves 4 to 6.

CAPPUCCINO PARFAITS

A winning and cool combination. Serve when a refreshing dessert is desired.

1 1/2 cups	Milk	375 mL
1	envelope unflavoured gelatin	1
1/4 cup	sugar	50 mL
2 tsp.	instant coffee granules	10 mL
2 cups	coffee ice cream	500 mL
1/4 cup	coffee liqueur	50 mL
	whipped cream	
	cinnamon	

1. Measure Milk in a 2 cup (500 mL) glass measure. Sprinkle gelatin over Milk and let stand 5 minutes to soften.

2. Stir mixture and microwave, uncovered, at High (100%) for 2 to 3 minutes or until gelatin is completely dissolved. Stir to help the granules dissolve. Stir in sugar and coffee granules until dissolved.

3. In a large bowl, break up ice cream. Pour gelatin mixture over ice cream and stir until ice cream is melted. Add liqueur.

4. Pour into four 8 oz. (250 mL) parfait glasses and chill until firm.

5. To serve, garnish with whipped cream and sprinkle with cinnamon.

Makes 4 servings.

CREAMY LIME AND
CHOCOLATE CRUMB PARFAITS

Lime and chocolate are such a delicious combination. This refreshing but creamy mixture is topped with slightly crunchy chocolate crumbs.

1/2 cup	sugar	125 mL
1/4 cup	cornstarch	50 mL
1 1/2 cups	Milk	375 mL
	grated peel of 1 lime	
1/2 cup	lime juice	125 mL
1 tsp.	vanilla	5 mL
	green food colouring	
2 tbsp.	butter	25 mL
3/4 cup	chocolate wafer or chocolate graham crumbs	175 mL
1/2 cup	whipping cream	125 mL

1. Combine sugar and cornstarch in an 8 cup (2 L) glass measure or microwavable bowl. Gradually whisk in Milk until smooth. Microwave, uncovered, at High (100%) for 3 to 5 minutes or until mixture comes to a boil and thickens. Whisk every 2 minutes. Mixture will be quite thick.

2. Stir in lime peel, lime juice and vanilla. Tint with green food colouring and set aside to cool to room temperature.

3. Meanwhile in a 2 cup (500 mL) microwavable bowl, melt butter at High (100%) for 40 to 60 seconds. Stir in crumbs until evenly combined. Spoon about 2 tbsp. (30 mL) crumbs in the bottom of four–8 oz. (250 mL) wine or parfait glasses. Reserve remaining crumbs for top. Flatten slightly with a spoon and set aside.

4. Whip cream until stiff. Fold into lime mixture. Divide lime mixture between prepared glasses. Sprinkle remaining crumbs on top of each parfait.

5. Chill until serving.

Serves 4.

BAKED LEMON SPONGE

This is a meringue baked over a light lemon custard. Make just before serving in order to serve warm.

2 tbsp.	butter	30	mL
1/2 cup	sugar	125	mL
3	eggs, separated	3	
	grated peel of 1/2 lemon		
1/4 cup	flour	50	mL
1/4 tsp.	salt	1	mL
1 cup	Milk	250	mL
1/4 cup	lemon juice	50	mL
2 tbsp.	sugar	30	mL

1. Cream butter, 1/2 cup (125 mL) sugar, egg yolks and lemon peel together until light. Combine flour and salt and add alternately to creamed mixture with Milk until smooth. Add lemon juice.

2. Beat egg whites until frothy. Gradually beat in 2 tbsp. (30 mL) sugar and beat until stiff but not dry. Gently fold into lemon mixture. Pour into a 4 cup (1 L) round microwavable casserole or bowl.

3. Microwave, uncovered, at Medium (50%) for 6 to 10 minutes or until top is set. Rotate casserole, as necessary, during cooking. Let stand for 5 minutes before serving.

4. To serve, spoon out meringue topping, then spoon lemon sauce over each serving. Serve warm.

Serves 4 to 6.

RAISIN AND BREAD PUDDING

This traditional family favourite is best served warm.

1 tbsp.	butter	15 mL
3 tbsp.	graham crumbs, divided	45 mL
1 1/2 cups	Milk	375 mL
2	eggs	2
1/2 cup	sugar	125 mL
1 tbsp.	rum or brandy, optional	15 mL
1 tsp.	vanilla	5 mL
6	slices bread, cut into 1 inch (2.5 cm) cubes	6
1/2 cup	raisins	125 mL
1/2 tsp.	cinnamon	2 mL

1. Butter a 4 cup (1 L) round microwavable casserole with butter. Sprinkle with 1 tbsp. (15 mL) of the graham crumbs and set aside.

2. Measure Milk into a 2 cup (500 mL) glass measure and microwave at High (100%) for 2 minutes or until hot but not boiling.

3. Meanwhile, whisk eggs and sugar together in a 4 cup (1 L) glass measure or microwavable bowl. Stir in rum or brandy, if using, and vanilla. Gradually whisk in hot Milk until smooth. Microwave, uncovered, at Medium (50%) for 2 to 3 minutes or until warmed. Add bread cubes and raisins, pushing bread cubes into liquid. Let stand for 5 minutes for bread to soak up some of the liquid.

4. Meanwhile, combine remaining 2 tbsp. (30 mL) of graham crumbs and cinnamon for topping, set aside.

5. Pour bread mixture into prepared dish. Sprinkle evenly with cinnamon crumbs. Cover with waxed paper and microwave at Medium (50%) for 8 to 12 minutes or until set and lightly puffed. Rotate casserole, as necessary, during cooking. A knife inserted in several places should come out clean. Let stand, uncovered, for 10 minutes. Serve warm.

Serves 4 to 6.

LUSCIOUS LEMON CAKE

Since microwave cakes cook to the same colour as the batter, this cake is a bright yellow colour. If desired, dust finished cake with cinnamon or nutmeg. A 12 cup (3 L) microwavable ring mould is needed for this size of cake.

1	500 or 520 g package lemon cake mix	1	
1	113 g package lemon pie filling	1	
2 cups	Milk	500	mL
2	eggs	2	
1/2 cup	sugar	125	mL
1/4 cup	lemon juice	50	mL

1. Combine cake mix, pie filling, Milk and eggs in a large mixer bowl. Blend ingredients at low speed, then beat at medium speed of electric beater for 3 minutes.

2. Pour into lightly buttered 12 cup (3 L) microwavable ring mould. Microwave, uncovered, at Medium (50%) for 10 minutes. Rotate pan, if necessary and microwave at High (100%) for 5 to 8 minutes or until surface is dry and toothpick inserted in several places comes out clean. Let stand, uncovered, directly on counter for 10 minutes.

3. Run a knife along edges and invert cake onto a large plate.

4. Stir together sugar and lemon juice until sugar is almost dissolved. Spoon over warm cake. Cool before serving. Once cool, wrap well in plastic wrap to prevent cake from drying out.

Serves 12 to 16.

DOUBLE FUDGE CHOCOLATE CAKE

This double layer chocolate cake has a rich fudge icing made with both chocolate and cocoa. Even if you only have one cake dish, this bakes so quickly that you can bake the second layer while cooling the first layer.

2 cups	all purpose flour	500	mL
1/4 cup	unsweetened cocoa powder	50	mL
2 tsp.	baking powder	10	mL
1 tsp.	baking soda	5	mL
1/2 tsp.	salt	2	mL
1 cup	butter	250	mL
1 1/4 cups	sugar	300	mL
3	eggs	3	
1 tsp.	vanilla	5	mL
1 cup	Milk	250	mL

Icing

8 oz.	semi-sweet or bittersweet chocolate	240	g
1/4 cup	unsweetened cocoa powder	50	mL
3/4 cup	Milk	175	mL
1/2 cup	butter	125	mL
3 cups	sifted icing sugar	750	mL
1 1/2 tsp.	vanilla	7	mL

1. Line the bottoms of two 9 inch (23 cm) round microwavable cake dishes (with straight sides) with a circle of waxed paper.

2. Combine flour, cocoa, baking powder, baking soda and salt.

3. Cream butter, then add sugar and beat until light and fluffy. Add eggs, one at a time and beat well after each addition. Add vanilla.

4. Add flour mixture to butter mixture alternately with Milk, beginning and ending with flour mixture. Stir just until combined.

5. Divide batter between the two dishes, filling only half full. Microwave one cake at a time, uncovered, at Medium (50%) for 6 minutes, rotating dish, as necessary, partway through cooking. Microwave at High (100%) for 2 to 5 minutes or until surface is nearly dry. A toothpick inserted in several places should come out clean. Repeat with second layer. (If you have one dish, cool, turn out cake and clean dish. Add a new circle of waxed paper, remaining cake batter and microwave as above.)

Continued on next page

DOUBLE FUDGE CHOCOLATE CAKE
(Continued)

6. Let stand, uncovered, directly on counter for 10 minutes. Run a knife around edge of cake and turn out onto a serving plate. Remove waxed paper and let cool completely before icing.

7. To make icing, combine chocolate, cocoa, Milk and butter in a large microwavable bowl. Microwave, uncovered, at High (100%) for 3 to 4 minutes or until melted. Stir partway through cooking and stir well at the end to help melting. Cool slightly. Beat in icing sugar and vanilla.

8. Refrigerate until spreadable, then spread between layers, top and sides.

Serves 8 to 12.

CRANBERRY NUT BREAD

A ring mould is the best shape for even cooking of quick breads. If you do not have a ring mould, use a 6 cup (1.5 L) microwavable casserole with a juice glass in the centre.

1 tbsp.	graham crumbs	15 mL
1/2 cup	butter, softened	125 mL
1/2 cup	dark brown sugar	125 mL
2	eggs	2
2 tsp.	grated orange peel	10 mL
1 1/2 cups	all purpose flour	375 mL
1 tsp.	baking powder	5 mL
1/2 tsp.	baking soda	2 mL
1/4 tsp.	salt	1 mL
1/2 cup	Milk	125 mL
1 cup	chopped cranberries	250 mL
1/2 cup	chopped nuts	125 mL

1. Butter a 6 cup (1.5 L) microwavable ring mould. Sprinkle with graham crumbs and set aside.

2. Cream butter and sugar until light. Beat in eggs, one at a time, then orange peel.

3. Combine flour, baking powder, baking soda and salt. Add flour mixture to butter mixture alternately with Milk, beginning and ending with flour mixture. Stir just until combined.

4. Stir in cranberries and nuts. Spoon into prepared ring mould. Microwave, uncovered, at Medium (50%) for 6 minutes. Rotate dish, if necessary and microwave at High (100%) for 3 to 5 minutes or until surface is dry and a toothpick inserted in several places comes out clean. Let stand, uncovered, directly on counter for 10 minutes.

5. Run a knife along the edges of cake and turn out onto a large plate. Cool completely before serving.

6. Once cool, wrap well with plastic wrap to prevent cake from drying out.

Serves 8 to 10.

HONEY PECAN COFFEE CAKE

The streusel topping gives an attractive colour and cinnamon flavour to this moist cake. Enjoy with coffee or tea.

Topping

1/2 cup	chopped pecans	125	mL
1/2 cup	packed brown sugar	125	mL
1 tsp.	cinnamon	5	mL

Cake

1/2 cup	Milk	125	mL
1 tbsp.	lemon juice	15	mL
1/2 cup	butter, softened	125	mL
1/2 cup	honey	125	mL
2	eggs	2	
1/2 tsp.	vanilla	2	mL
1 1/2 cups	all purpose flour	375	mL
1 1/2 tsp.	baking powder	7	mL
1/2 tsp.	baking soda	2	mL
1/4 tsp.	salt	1	mL

1. Butter a 6 cup (1.5 L) microwavable ring mould. Combine topping ingredients and sprinkle half in ring mould. Set aside.

2. Combine Milk and lemon juice, set aside.

3. Cream butter with honey until light. Beat in eggs, one at a time, then vanilla.

4. Combine flour, baking powder, baking soda and salt. Add flour mixture to butter mixture alternately with Milk mixture, beginning and ending with flour mixture. Beat just until combined.

5. Spoon half the batter into ring mould. Sprinkle with remaining topping mixture, then remaining batter.

6. Microwave, uncovered, at Medium (50%) for 6 minutes. Rotate dish, if necessary, and microwave at High (100%) for 3 to 5 minutes or until surface is dry and a toothpick inserted in several places comes out clean. Let stand, directly on counter for 10 minutes.

7. Run a knife along the edges of cake and turn out onto a large plate.

8. Serve warm. Once cool, wrap well in plastic wrap to prevent cake from drying out.

Serves 8 to 10.

MAPLE FUDGE TARTS

These buttery maple tarts are delightfully rich, so make them small. Use frozen tart shells to save time, but bake them conventionally before making filling.

16-18	2 inch (5 cm) baked tart shells	16–18
1/4 cup	butter	50 mL
1/3 cup	cornstarch	75 mL
1 cup	maple syrup	250 mL
1/2 cup	Milk	125 mL
	toasted almond slices, optional	

1. Melt butter in a 4 cup (1 L) glass measure at High (100%) for 1 to 1 1/2 minutes. Blend in cornstarch. Whisk in maple syrup and Milk until smooth. Microwave, uncovered, at High (100%) for 3 to 5 minutes or until mixture comes to a boil and thickens. Whisk twice during cooking.

2. Let cool for 15 minutes. Spoon into cooled, baked shells. Allow to completely cool. (The filling will firm up as it cools.) Garnish with toasted almond slices, if desired.

Makes 16 to 18 tarts.

EASY RAISIN RICE PUDDING

This simple rice pudding is quickly made with cooked rice and a pudding mix.

1	4 serving size package vanilla pudding and pie filling	1
2 1/2 cups	Milk	625 mL
3/4 cup	raisins	175 mL
2 cups	cooked rice*	500 mL
1/2 tsp.	vanilla	2 mL
	cinnamon and nutmeg	

1. Whisk pudding mix and Milk together in an 8 cup (2 L) glass measure until smooth. Microwave, uncovered, at High (100%) for 5 to 8 minutes or until mixture comes to a boil and thickens. Whisk every 2 minutes.

2. Cool slightly, then stir in raisins, rice and vanilla. Season to taste with cinnamon and nutmeg. Serve warm or cooled.

Serves 6 to 8.

*For 2 cups (500 mL) cooked rice, combine 3/4 cup (175 mL) long grain rice and 1 1/2 cups (375 mL) water in an 8 cup (2 L) microwavable casserole. Cover and microwave at High (100%) for 5 minutes. Reduce to Medium (50%) for 10 to 14 minutes or until most of the liquid is absorbed. Let stand, covered, for 10 to 15 minutes to absorb remaining liquid.

Send order forms to: The Ontario Milk Marketing Board
                        Milk's Microwave Cookbook Offer
                        P. O. Box 812, Dept. B
                        Belleville, Ontario
                        K8N 5B5

Give your friends their very own copy of Milk's Microwave Cookbook.

Please send _____ cookbook(s) to:

Name: _____

Street: _____   Apt. Number: _____

City: _____   Province: _____   Postal Code: _____

I am enclosing $9.95 for each cookbook ordered to cover cost, postage
and handling.

Enclosed is: _____   Signed: _____

Prices are subject to change after November 30, 1990

Give your friends their very own copy of Milk's Microwave Cookbook.

Please send _____ cookbook(s) to:

Name: _____

Street: _____   Apt. Number: _____

City: _____   Province: _____   Postal Code: _____

I am enclosing $9.95 for each cookbook ordered to cover cost, postage
and handling.

Enclosed is: _____   Signed: _____

Prices are subject to change after November 30, 1990

Send order forms to: The Ontario Milk Marketing Board
                         Cook Milk In Any Flavour You Like
                         Cookbook Offer
                         P. O. Box 812, Dept. B
                         Belleville, Ontario
                         K8N 5B5

**Get cooking
with a
Canadian
bestseller!**

Over 600 delicious recipes, organized into
6 easy reference sections. From soups and
appetizers to entrées and desserts, an
absolute must for every cook!

I love to Cook! Please send _____ cookbook(s) to:

Name: _____

Street: _____   Apt. Number: _____

City: _____   Province: _____   Postal Code: _____

I am enclosing $10.95 for each cookbook ordered to cover cost, postage and
handling.

Enclosed is: _____   Signed: _____

Prices are subject to change after November 30, 1990

**Get cooking
with a
Canadian
bestseller!**
Over 600 delicious recipes, organized into
6 easy reference sections. From soups and
appetizers to entrées and desserts, an
absolute must for every cook!

I love to Cook! Please send _____ cookbook(s) to:

Name: _____

Street: _____   Apt. Number: _____

City: _____   Province: _____   Postal Code: _____

I am enclosing $10.95 for each cookbook ordered to cover cost, postage and
handling.

Enclosed is: _____   Signed: _____

Prices are subject to change after November 30, 1990
